MORRIS VENDEN

GOD SAYS,

BUT I THINK

D1510758

MORRIS VENDEN

GOD SAYS,

BUT I THINK

Has God's Word taken
a back seat to our opinion?

Pacific Press Publishing Association
Boise, Idaho
Oshawa, Ontario, Canada

Edited by Marvin Moore
Designed by Dennis Ferree
Cover photo by Betty Blue
Typeset in 11/13 Century Schoolbook

Library of Congress Cataloging-in-Publication Data:
Venden, Morris L.
    God says, but I think / Morris Venden
            p.   cm.
    ISBN 0-8163-1137-4
    1. Christian life—1960- 2. Venden, Morris L. I. Title.
    BV4501.2.V384   1993
    248.4—dc20   92-36874
                                                       CIP

93 94 95 96 97 ● 5 4 3 2 1

Contents

God Says,
but I Think

Chapter 1

God Says,
but I Think

*P*erhaps you heard about the preacher who traveled to San Francisco to cry out against the abominations done there. He walked along I-80 to the Bay Bridge and across. After he'd completed his mission, he came back a different direction. Coming out through Pleasant Hill and down I-680 he crossed the Benicia Bridge, because he had been told he was to return a different way than the way he went.

Although he wasn't supposed to stop for refreshment along the way, he did pause at a local pancake house to pick up some buckwheat pancakes. Before he ordered them, another preacher from the Bay Area met him and accosted him, saying, "Aren't you the one who was speaking out against certain things in San Francisco today?"

"Yes, I am the one."

"Well, come home with me," the second preacher said. "I am a preacher too. Come home, and I will give you dinner and some Kool-Aid."

The first preacher said that he could not go, but the second preacher kept insisting, so the first preacher went.

But things didn't turn out too well. After dinner, the preacher from the Bay Area loaned the first preacher his new Chrysler Cordoba, and on the way back there was a terrible head-on collision on the freeway. The first preacher lost his life. Ultimately, both preachers were buried in the same cemetery side by side.

Any similarity between that story and 1 Kings 13 might be coincidental. But I would like to remind you of this ancient story, because it challenges us to depend only on God for truth, through our own study and prayer. It teaches us not to depend on anyone else, even a "man of God."

Solomon was gone, and Rehoboam had taken the throne. But he accepted the wrong counsel because he turned to the wrong people for advice. As a result there was rebellion. Ten tribes withdrew, seceding from the union, and they appointed Jeroboam as their king. So Rehoboam was left with only two tribes out of the twelve.

Jeroboam had been an officer under Solomon, but he got into trouble and fled as a fugitive to Egypt. While there, he learned about some of the gods and customs of the Egyptians. Later, when he found himself king of the ten northern tribes, Jeroboam feared that the people of the northern kingdom, because of their long custom, would travel to Jerusalem to worship God. He feared that their hearts would be drawn back to what was now known as the kingdom of Judah. So he set up new days, new dates, new times, and new places to worship God. One of these was in Dan and the other in Bethel. He did not choose the priests as God had directed. Rather, he chose them from the lowest of the people. He even appointed himself as one of them. One day Jeroboam was standing at this altar in Bethel to offer sacrifice when a voice stopped him. First Kings 13 describes what happened.

> Behold, there came a man of God out of Judah by the word of the Lord unto Bethel: and Jeroboam stood by the altar to burn incense. And he cried against the altar by the word of the Lord, and said, O altar, altar, thus saith the Lord; Behold, a child shall be born unto

the house of David, Josiah by name; and upon thee shall he offer the priests of the high places that burn incense upon thee, and men's bones shall be burnt upon thee (1 Kings 13:1, 2).

This prophecy was made 300 years before it took place! Although some people say that prophecy and its fulfillment are subject to chance and coincidence, it's rather difficult to allow that when you have a detailed prophecy like this, including the name of the man and precisely what he was going to do. It's one thing to say, "It's going to rain sometime during the year three hundred." It's quite another thing to give details like this.

Verse 3 says:

He gave a sign the same day, saying, This is the sign which the Lord hath spoken; Behold, the altar shall be rent, and the ashes that are upon it shall be poured out. And it came to pass, when King Jeroboam heard the saying of the man of God, which had cried against the altar in Bethel, that he put forth his hand from the altar, saying, Lay hold on him. And his hand, which he put forth against him, dried up, so that he could not pull it in again to him. The altar also was rent, and the ashes poured out from the altar, according to the sign which the man of God had given by the word of the Lord.

You'll have to admit that it must have been rather exciting to stand in the crowd that day. How would you have felt being there with such strange things happening?

Verse 6 begins to give the picture of an apparently repentant king. "The king answered and said unto the man of God, Intreat now the face of the Lord thy God, and pray for me, that my hand may be restored me again." You'd "repent," too, if you were in that kind of a predicament, wouldn't you? He should have prayed for a new heart instead of a new hand. "And the man of God besought the Lord, and the king's hand was restored him again, and became as it was before."

Now the king became very friendly: "And the king said unto the man of God, Come home with me, and refresh thyself, and I will give thee a reward. And the man of God said unto the king, If thou wilt give me half thine house, I will not go in with thee, neither will I eat bread nor drink water in this place" (verses 7, 8). Obviously, the king, whose heart was still the same, wanted the man of God to condone his devious actions. If in the eyes of the people the man of God had conceded to the king's dinner invitation, it would have looked like the king was in good standing again, which he wasn't.

The man of God explained why he could not accept the king's hospitality: "For so was it charged me by the word of the lord, saying, Eat no bread, nor drink water, nor turn again by the same way that thou camest. So he went another way, and returned not by the way that he came to Bethel" (verse 9). In verse 11 the plot thickens:

Now there dwelt an old prophet in Bethel; and his sons came and told him all the works that the man of God had done that day in Bethel: the words which he had spoken unto the king, them they told also to their father. And their father said unto them, What way went he? For his sons had seen what way the man of God went, which came from Judah. And he said unto his sons, Saddle me the ass. So they saddled him the ass: and he rode thereon, and went after the man of God, and found him sitting under an oak (verses 11-14).

Could he have been sitting there, thinking of the reward that he had missed out on?

And he said unto him, Art thou the man of God that camest from Judah? And he said, I am. Then he said unto him, Come home with me, and eat bread. And he said, I may not return with thee, nor go in with thee: neither will I eat bread nor drink water with thee in this place: For it was said to me by the word of the Lord, Thou shalt eat no bread nor drink water there, nor turn again to go by the way that thou camest. He said unto him, I am a prophet also as thou art; and an angel spake unto me by the word of the Lord, saying, Bring him back with thee into thine house, that he may eat bread and drink water. But he lied unto him. So he went back with him, and did eat bread in his house, and drank water (verses 14-19).

Here we see the crux of the matter. Even godly men sometimes give in to this crippling dependence upon another person. But it only makes sense to us in the twentieth century, doesn't it, that if the angel who sent the first prophet down to Bethel had had a change of plans, he would have told the man of God himself?

I once had a woman call me up and ask me to go to Alaska with her. She said it had been revealed to her by the Lord that there were gold nuggets up there. All you had to do was take a broom, sweep off the snow, and pick them up. She claimed that this would be a great advance for the Lord's work. It had all been revealed to her.

I said, "When the Lord reveals that to me, we'll go." I said that on the basis of the story we've just been talking about. Don't take what someone else comes along and tells you, even though they bring the Lord into it. Verse 20 says:

As they sat at the table, . . . the word of the Lord came unto the prophet that brought him back: And he cried unto the man of God that came from Judah, saying, Thus saith the lord, Forasmuch as thou hast disobeyed the mouth of the Lord, and hast not kept the commandment which the Lord thy God commanded thee, but camest back, and hast eaten bread and drunk water in the place, of the which the Lord did say to thee, Eat no bread, and drink no water; thy carcase shall not come unto the sepulchre of thy fathers (verses 20-22).

It was very important to be buried in the family sepulchre in those days. So this was a dire prediction.

And it came to pass, after he had eaten bread, and after he had drunk, that he saddled for him the ass, to wit, for the prophet whom he had brought back. And when he was gone, a lion met him by the way, and slew him: and his carcase was cast in the way, and the ass stood by it, the lion also stood by the carcase. And behold, men passed by, and saw the carcase cast in the way, and the lion standing by the carcase: and they came and told it in the city where the old prophet dwelt. And when the prophet that brought him back from the way heard thereof, he said, It is the man of God, who was disobedient unto the word of the Lord: therefore the Lord hath delivered him unto the lion, which hath torn him, and slain him, according to the word of the Lord, which he spake unto him.

And he spake to his sons, saying, Saddle me the ass. And they saddled him. And he went and found his carcase cast in the way, and the ass and the lion standing by the carcase: the lion had not eaten the carcase, nor torn the ass. And the prophet took up the carcase of the man of God, and laid it upon the ass, and brought it back: and the old prophet came to the city, to mourn and to bury him. And he laid his carcase in his own grave; and they mourned over him, saying, Alas, my brother! And it came to pass, after he had buried him, that he spake to his sons, saying, When I am dead, then bury me in the sepulchre wherein the man of God is buried, lay my bones beside his bones: For the saying which he cried by the word of the Lord against the altar in Bethel, and against all the houses of the high places which are in the cities of Samaria, shall surely come to pass (verses 23-32).

And it did. Let's consider the tragedy of the matter. Back in the Garden of Eden, you see two people who have been told something by the Lord. They knew what God said, but they thought their way would be all right.

"God says, but I think I'll do it my way."

You see a golden calf on the plains in the wilderness, and the people have only recently heard a warning against it from the mouth of God Himself. But they said, "We know what God said, but we think it'll be all right."

You see Ananias and Sapphira, who knew about God's warning against false witness, but they thought it would be all right to tell a falsehood to the apostles. You see Uzzah, who, with others, had been told to keep his hands off the ark. But he said, "I think it'll be all right."

You see a boy walking down the furrow on a hot summer day, like Uncle Arthur used to tell us, and he's been promised he can go swimming after he has all the pumpkin seeds planted. He's supposed to put in three seeds and walk two paces, put in three seeds and walk two paces. But he put in a handful every two paces instead. He forgot about the law of the harvest. He thought, "It'll be all right." Later, when he realized what he'd done, he prayed that the Lord would kill some of those seeds. But the law continued.

You see a person involved in a death sport. He's going to defy gravity. He knows the law of gravity, but he thinks he will make it through. He'll be safe. And you see a man coming home from Bethel. He knows what God has said, but he thinks . . . The old prophet made two mistakes. First, he depended on his own wisdom, and second, this resulted in dependence on another person.

I'd like you to notice a few lessons in this graphic story. The first one is that a man of God can slip. Some people say a man of God can fall. Did he fall, or did he slip? That depends on how you read it. There are two ways to read the Bible. There's the intellectual way (which becomes the pseudointellectual way). "Scriptural difficulties can never be mastered by the same methods that are employed in grappling with philosophical problems. . . . An understanding of Bible truth depends not so much upon the power of intellect brought to the search as on the singleness of purpose, the earnest longing after righteousness" (*The Great Controversy*, p. 599).

If I were to take the intellectual, philosophical approach to this story, I'd say, How come a poor man of God, who slips because he's thirsty, gets eaten by a lion on the way home; and Jeroboam, who, in my opinion, should have been wiped out by ten lions, goes scot-free? Is that a fair question? Intellectually, it appears to be grossly unfair. Jeroboam was king of ten tribes in Israel. His hand withered up, and all he had to do was make a simple request, and his hand was healed again. But the man of God got killed by a lion. If I approached it on a purely intellectual basis, I'd have to say, That's what I've been looking for—a good reason to forget the Bible and God and faith and the church and religion. Forget the whole thing, and become a cynic and a skeptic.

How do you handle questions like that?

Here's how I do it. I settled in my mind a long time ago that God is fair and just. He always has been, and He always will be. Does that sound naïve? Have you settled this in your thinking? And if there's any lack, can you trust that it's on your part, not God's part? If I've already settled that, on the basis of studying the whole picture, then I can approach this story knowing that God is love, that He loves me, and that He loved both of these people. Am I seeking a reason to doubt the Bible, or am I seeking a reason to find the truth God has for me in this story?

The doubter could take another look at this and say, "Even though he was a man of God, God was just waiting for an opportunity to kill him."

That would be like some children at junior camp thought. They were jumping on the trampoline before sundown on Sabbath, when one of the girls slipped and broke her leg. On the way to the hospital the campers said, "If we hadn't jumped on the trampoline before sundown, God wouldn't have broken her leg." In other words, God is looking for legs to break! Watch out!

I'd like to quote something from *Thoughts From the Mount of Blessing*:

> It is not safe for us to linger to contemplate the advantages to be reaped through yielding to Satan's suggestions. Sin means dishonor and disaster to every soul that indulges in it; but it is blinding and deceiving in its nature, and it will entice us with flattering presentations. If we venture on Satan's ground we have no assurance of protection from his power (p. 118).

I don't believe God killed the prophet. I believe He accepted the only alternative He had. When the prophet chose to disobey, God had to let the devil do whatever the devil wanted to do with him. *I believe the devil killed him.* The Bible says it was a lion. Who is it that walks around like a roaring lion, seeking whom he may devour? (See 1 Peter 5:8.) If I were Satan, I would say, "Look at these kids jumping before sundown! If I break one of their legs, they'll blame God." And if I want people to blame God, I would be happy for the opportunity.

I believe Satan was responsible for the man of God's death. God doesn't crowd us with His protection. If we choose to go apart from Him, we forfeit His protection, not because *He* wants us to, but because *we* want to.

This brings us to another question. Does this mean that the man of God was eternally lost? Did this experience seal his destiny forever? On first glance, most of us, if we were asked, would say, "Oh yes, he's had it. No chance for him." That's based on the old idea that if you slip or fail and then die before you have a chance to confess your sin, you are lost forever. I'm not sure we can take this position about the man of God. I don't know of any place where it tells us he was lost forever, nor does it say he was saved forever. But I do know that the book *Steps to Christ* says our character is not determined by the occasional good deed or misdeed, but by the tendency of the life, the direction in which our life is going (see *Steps to Christ*, pp. 57, 58).

I also know that Moses was a man of God. He slipped, and he forfeited translation. Why? Because it's a serious thing for someone who is a spokesperson for God to be a wrong example and influence while delivering a message from God. But Moses, if I understand it correctly, is in heaven right now. I am not going to put this other man of God in heaven, but I am unwilling, on the basis of what I know about God, to say that he was eternally lost.

Another point we find through this story is that God sometimes talks through liars. This is an interesting concept, isn't it? But it's true. God speaks through whomever

He will. Jesus said that if the children and others had not sung praises on the day of the triumphal entry, the stones would have (see Luke 19:40). God has even talked through donkeys. So let's not put it past Him to speak a message through a liar, even though that seems rather unusual.

Then we come to the major point in this story: The one who is deceived by someone else is held accountable for being deceived. I used to listen to an evangelist who asked, "If a man is deceived by a false prophet, will God hold the false prophet responsible and allow the man who was deceived to go free?" The answer, of course, was No. The one who is deceived is responsible himself.

Someone says, "I know a Bible instructor who is teaching error in one of our institutions, and this is going to cause people to be lost." I don't believe that. Everyone who is lost will be lost as a result of his or her own choice, and it will be his or her own fault. We choose to be deceived.

Let me quote it to you from *The Great Controversy*: "The spirit of God is freely bestowed to enable every man to lay hold upon the means of salvation. . . . Men fail of salvation through their own willful refusal of the gift of life" (p. 262). "But," we say, "someday people are going to stand up in the judgment and point their fingers at us and say, 'I'm lost, and you knew something, and you didn't tell me.' "

Yes, that may happen. But their argument isn't going to be worth a penny. Because on the basis of this story, I can tell you that people are lost by their own choice. People are deceived by their own decision.

Oh, but we hear about the day coming when people will suddenly wake up to the realization that they have been deceived. Then they're going to turn against their ministers, their teachers, and their leaders, and they will tear them limb from limb.

Yes, but that's only a projection of their own problem. The reason anyone is deceived is that he doesn't search and study and find out for himself.

Here's a parable that addresses this idea that people are saved or lost because of our influence, and therefore it's our responsibility. You are walking from San Francisco to Pacific Union College, the Promised Land. As you walk along, someone comes by and says, "Where are you going?"

You say, "I'm going to the Promised Land."

"That's where I'm going," your new friend exclaims. "Get in the car, and I'll take you." So you get in the car with him. Now you get to Pacific Union College sooner than you would have. This person saved you a lot of blisters and perspiration, and he had a part in your getting there. *But you were going to get there anyway!*

Let's change it. Now you're walking from San Francisco to Reno (the other place). Presently someone comes by in a car and says, "Where are you going?"

You say, "I'm going to Reno."

Your new friend says, "That's where I am going. Get in, and I'll help you get there." So you got there sooner. And this "kind" person had a part in your getting there. *But that's where you were going anyway!*

I've had theologians come to me and say, "We object to your parable. Suppose that you were walking to Reno, and you *thought* you were going to Pacific Union College."

The quotation we just read answers this point: "The Spirit of God is freely bestowed to enable every man to lay hold upon the means of salvation. . . . Men fail of salvation through their own willful refusal of the gift of life" (ibid.).

Another objection is this: Suppose that you are on your way to Pacific Union College and someone comes along and says, "Why don't you go to Reno?" That's precisely what this story is about, isn't it? This person deceived you into going to Reno instead of Pacific Union College, because he convinced you that going to Reno was better. But you are still responsible, according to our story in the Bible.

What am I saying? That God has made each person his or her own pope, and that it is the responsibility of each of us to search, dig, pray, and study for ourselves. No one can search and pray and study and dig for another. It cannot be done any more than we can eat for another or sleep for another.

A story is told about a man who worried all the time. He worried so much that his friends began to worry about his worrying. Then one day one of his friends met him on the street and discovered that the man had ceased worrying. "What has happened?" the friend asked.

"I quit worrying," the man said.

"How did you do that?" his friend asked.

"I hired someone to do my worrying for me."

"What do you pay him?"

"I pay him one thousand dollars a month."

"How can you afford that?"

"I can't," the ex-worrier said. "That's the first thing he has to worry about."

When I heard this story, I thought it was a good joke. It's funny because it's so ridiculous. But we take the same thing and transfer it over to the realm of religion, and then we think it's OK. Although we don't say so, we often find it easy to depend on someone else to do our studying (our eating) and our praying (our breathing) for us. And we don't think that's funny. We think it's all right, it's real, it's normal. We think this is acceptable. Yet it's just as foolish as letting someone worry for us.

It's possible to be so brilliant, so educated, and so sophisticated that we think our opinion is worth something in terms of truth. Our opinion is worth nothing in terms of truth. God has revealed His truth, and we must all find it and accept it and know it for ourselves. Do you accept that? Or are you going to go on trying to judge truth on the basis of someone else—the one who has the nicest personality or who is the fastest talker?

The line is drawn between those who trust human authority and those who accept no authority except God's Word, searched out, digested, and studied for themselves. God says, but I think.

God says, but *he* thinks. God says, but *somebody else* thinks. Have you heard what *he* thinks, what *they* think? What they think means nothing!

And this works in another area as well. Someone may say, "I know that God says,'Come unto me, all ye that labor and are heavy laden, and I will give you rest' (Matthew 11:28). But I can't come to Him because I'm too bad. I'll have to change my life in order to come to Him. But if I have to change my life to come to Him, I'll never get there."

That's right! When Jesus says, "Come unto me, all ye that labor and are heavy laden," don't go adding what you think. His invitation still stands. Doesn't it?

Someone says, "I know that Isaiah says, 'Though your sins be as scarlet, they shall be as white as snow' (Isaiah 1:18). But mine are too scarlet. There's no chance for me. I know what God said, but I think it won't happen to *me*."

It makes no difference what you think. God still says it. Aren't you thankful for that? Jesus said, "I, if I be lifted up from the earth, will draw all men unto me" (John 12:32).

And they say, "How can it be that everywhere throughout this world, wherever the cross of Christ is lifted up, all people are being drawn, whether they accept or not?"

Jesus made it clear that the Holy Spirit is working on every heart.

But you say, "Not so with me! He's left me! I think . . ."

No, don't go by what you *think*. Remember Jesus' invitation through His Spirit. It is what God says.

So I appeal to you to trust God. Believe what He says, and know that He'll do what is best for you. And remember to thank Him for leading you and guiding you in your life up to this point. If you ask Him to, He will lead forever.

People-Centered People

Chapter 2

People-Centered People

A friend of mine went to visit a friend of his one day. He found him out in his shop working with a big hammer. So my friend, deciding to be a bit adventurous, put his thumb on the workbench and said, "Hit my thumb." The man with the hammer thought he would pull his thumb away, and the man with the thumb didn't think he would hit it. There was a gross misunderstanding, and my friend went off to the doctor with a thumb that looked like a piece of hamburger. I told this story one time, and someone said that he tried that with his expensive watch and got the same result. He ended up with a piece of tin foil for a watch.

People depending on people can be a real problem. In fact, I would like to address this question, because it seems to me that it's a very practical way to consider what our authority is for what we believe and do. Do we depend on people for our beliefs? Do we depend on certain leaders or certain charismatic types who know how to influence the masses to tell us what to do? What is the authority for why you think the way you think? What is the basis for your choice of actions?

In the days of Christ there was a heavy debate about this. It was common in those days to ask, "Who has believed?" "Which of the leaders has accepted?"

The Jewish spy ring had been out doing their homework. They were trying to trap Jesus. The leaders who sent them were disappointed when they came back without Him. "Then came the officers to the chief priests and Pharisees; and they said unto them, Why have ye not brought him? The officers answered, Never man spake like this man. Then answered them the Pharisees, Are ye also deceived? Have any of the rulers or of the Pharisees believed on him?" (John 7:45-48).

Evidently this disease has plagued the church for a long, long time! And it did not begin in the days of Christ. There is a certain Old Testament passage that almost sounds unbelievable. It could make you paranoid. It might even make you suspicious of everybody. "Trust ye not in a friend," it says.

You mean we're not supposed to trust our friends?

"Put ye not confidence in a guide: keep the doors of thy mouth from her that lieth in thy bosom."

Even someone *that* close to you?

"For the son dishonoreth the father, the daughter riseth up against her mother, the daughter-in-law against her mother-in-law; a man's enemies are the people of his own house" (Micah 7:5-7).

There was a little boy who spent time reading his scrolls around the hills of Nazareth as He was growing up. Later He remembered this passage from the Old Testament. His name was Jesus. What do you learn from this kind of information from the Old Testament and from the New Testament—to be careful whom you trust? Do you learn not to trust anybody? What does the psalmist mean when he says, "It is better to trust in the Lord than to put confidence in man" (Psalm 118:8)? What does it mean in Psalm 146:3, 4: "Put not your trust in princes, nor in the son of man, in whom there is no help. His breath goeth forth, he returneth to his earth; in that very day his thoughts perish"? What did Paul mean when he said, "Stop saying I am a follower of Paul, I am a follower of Apollos, I am a follower of Peter" (1 Corinthians 3:4, paraphrased)? What were these Bible writers getting at? Where do we draw the line?

Well, we don't want to develop a crowd of people who don't trust anymore, although it is a rough time in which to trust. Back in the pioneer days, when people left on a vacation, they'd sometimes pin the money they owed someone on the front gate for their creditor to pick up a few days later. How times have changed! According to one report I read recently, 80 percent of those who go to a mechanic for services these days are going to get ripped off. It used to be that we could trust everybody until they proved they couldn't be trusted. Now we don't trust anybody until they prove they *can* be trusted. I don't like to live in a world like that.

So, what do all those Bible verses mean that tell us not to trust anyone? As I understand it within the context, the Bible means don't trust anyone for truth. Don't trust anyone else to do your spiritual thinking for you. Don't trust anyone with your eternal destiny. Make sure of your authority for what you believe and why you believe it. That's the message. I'd like to challenge you to consider this very carefully.

We live in a time when many people are ignorant and religiously naive. It's been proven again and again. Recently someone handed me this little story:

"The pastor visited a class of boys one Sunday morning to find out what they were learning during Bible study. 'Who broke down the walls of Jericho?' he asked.

" 'Not me, sir,' the boys replied.

" 'Is this typical for this class?' the pastor asked the teacher.

" 'These are honest boys, and I believe them,' the teacher replied. 'I don't believe they would do a thing like that.'

"Frustrated and discouraged, the pastor told the Sunday school director about his visit to the class and the response of the boys and their teacher.

" 'Pastor, I have known the teacher and those boys for a long time,' the director replied. 'If they said they didn't do it, that's good enough for me.'

"Next the minister brought the matter before the official board of the church. They discussed it for two hours, then reported: 'Pastor, we see no need to get upset about a little thing like this. Let's just pay for any damages involved and charge it to general church maintenance.' "

We live in a time of great naiveté about religious things, including knowledge of the Bible. People who wouldn't think of treating their business the way they treat God act as though they're not even using their minds at all.

A recent newspaper headline said, "Church sources hail the orders relaxing the rules." According to the article that followed, "American church sources say the relaxation of the regulations concerning communion fast and evening services should result in a new era of spirituality. The decree made clear that the new rules required abstinence from solid food and alcoholic drinks for only three hours before attending and receiving communion. In the past the precommunion fast began at midnight. So now people can drink nonalcoholic drinks up to three hours before the service and water anytime. And this," they said, "should result in a great new era of spirituality."

What kind of people can even read that kind of reporting and not be shocked? What kind of people can live in that kind of religious atmosphere unless they've been trained not to think? People get on airplanes with their laptop computers and their pocket calculators and their portfolios and attaché cases. They don't sleep, they don't visit, they work. They're on the upward mobility ladder. And they're treating their business with every ounce of energy and efficiency they have. But if people would treat their business the way they treat the things of God and faith and eternity, they would be bankrupt in a few weeks.

I guess I'm throwing out a challenge to all of us to make sure what the basis of our authority is. Are we really giving it careful thought?

Our church pioneers did a lot of thinking. Here is a sample of the kind of thing that some of them heard in those days. "Satan is constantly endeavoring to attract attention to man in the place of God. He leads the people to look to bishops, to pastors, to professors of theology, as their guides, instead of searching the Scriptures to learn . . . for themselves" (*The Great Controversy*, p. 595). Here's another sample: "The great danger with our people has been that of depending upon men and making flesh their arm. Those who have not been in the habit of searching the Bible for themselves, or weighing evidence, have confidence in the leading men." That's a shocker. Who does that? Let's finish that quote. "Those who have not been in the habit of searching the Bible for themselves, or weighing evidence, have confidence in the leading men and accept the decisions they make; and thus many will reject the very messages God sends to His people, if these leading brethren do not accept them" (*Testimonies to Ministers*, pp. 106, 107). Don't even trust in leaders for truth or things concerning your eternal destiny.

Then what are leaders for? What are preachers for? I often wonder about that! As I understand it, the leaders' job is to encourage and motivate people to study and search and think for themselves. People are not to believe anything that preachers say unless they have searched it out on their own and have come to their own conclusions.

I had a call one time from a distraught mother. One of her

children, an academy student, was having problems with big questions about faith and God, the Bible, and eternity. He quit going to church but was sitting up till midnight asking his mother all kinds of questions about these big issues. She didn't know what to say, so she came to me. I said, "Thank God for this challenge to your own thinking."

"Oh, but I can't give him the reasons," the mother said. "I just always believed this way."

That's not good enough, Mother! Thank God you have a boy who is at least asking questions, when so many others his age don't even care. And thank God for the opportunity to be driven to your knees to search for yourself to make sure you have the answers. Isn't that what the Bible is pleading with us to do?

And what about people who are afraid that someone will be led astray? Have you been apprehensive about certain institutions, certain churches—maybe some of our own schools, and some teachers who aren't exactly orthodox? Have you ever been in a situation like that? And have you worried?

I'd like to ask you plainly, where are you going to find *any* institution, or *anyone* who is infallible, no longer subject to error?

"Oh, H. M. S. Richards," you say.

Well, that would be an easy one to get me on.

"But can't I trust Graham Maxwell or Jack Provonsha or Billy Graham or Dobson?" you ask.

No. The Bible says, Don't trust anyone for truth unless you've searched it out for yourself.

Listen, here are a few one-liners that our pioneers used to repeat: "Trust in the wisdom of man does not facilitate growth in grace." "The mind that depends upon the judgment of others is certain, sooner or later, to be misled." "It is the work of true education to train the youth to be thinkers and not mere reflectors of other men's thoughts."

"Allow no one to be brains for you. Allow no one to do your thinking, your investigating and your praying." Don't do it.

Our pioneers used to get together in Hiram Edson's barn. Have you ever heard of Hiram Edson's barn? These were young people. They would spend time praying, searching, and studying. "But," someone says, "they had truth handed to them as a special gift."

No, they didn't. They studied and hammered away and prayed and sweated and fasted until they came up with great truth. Then it was confirmed or verified by the special gift. But they studied for themselves, and they came to their own conclusions about certain great truths that we still hold dear today.

Sometimes I wonder if we shouldn't have another Hiram Edson's barn today to grapple with some of the *experiential* issues that press us because they haven't been addressed as they should. One that I'd like to suggest is the question of divine power and human effort. Some of our greatest minds ought to be bent to study that one, because everybody is on his own on that subject. Confusion! What about the exercise of the will? Confusion! Am I lost every time I sin? Some say Yes, some say No. More confusion! What about the nature of Christ? That's a hot one. It is everywhere in the world. Should we get together in another Hiram Edson's barn, or maybe a condominium at Lake Tahoe? Shouldn't we get all the thinkers together and hammer it out so we have a consensus that we can print in the church paper? Or do we already know that this is hopeless? Maybe the only consensus we're going to get is from the private chambers where people meet in their closets on their knees. Perhaps, sooner or later, maybe in the mountains someday, when the final smoke is rising, God's people will discover that they have a consensus, because the same Spirit has been leading all of them.

Why is anyone deceived? Is it because we have too many

deceivers around? No, people are deceived because they choose to be deceived. Because they choose not to study and search for themselves.

Jesus knew that the only true learning and acceptance of truth came from people studying and searching for themselves. That's why He was the Master Teacher. He did not give pat answers. He knew that no one is ever taught anything. People are only led to an atmosphere where they discover for themselves. Through the apostle Paul He made it clear that we should study to show ourselves approved unto God (see 2 Timothy 2:15).

Martin Luther came up with these famous premises: justification by faith, not by works; *sola Scriptura* (the Bible only); and the priesthood of all believers—everyone his own pope. If I were to ask whether you are a Catholic, a Protestant, or a Jew, most of those reading this book would say, "I am a Protestant."

My question to you is, What are you protesting?

"I beg your pardon," you say. "Am I supposed to be protesting something?"

Yes, that's what a Protestant is—one who protests something. Check it out, please, and find out what it is you are protesting.

When Luther threw his bombshell into the religious system of his day, he was simply calling for something that the early church called for again and again. That's why the New Testament says the people in Berea were more noble than those in Thessalonica. *They searched the Word daily*, to find out whether these things were so (see Acts 17:11).

We could make a strong appeal for making sure we have a solid base for our authority, and people could say, "Amen, I believe that, in theory." But, I'd like to suggest that the only person who really believes it in experience is the one who enters into that experience of what he teaches with

Christ Himself. Because if I am not in a vital relationship with Jesus, then I am going to depend upon people.

If I have a good image of myself and am a little arrogant and self-sufficient, I'll depend on myself, and I will qualify for what the Bible calls a "fool." He that trusteth in his own heart (or mind) is a fool (see Proverbs 28:26). Or, if I have a low image of myself and I'm not self-confident, and if I am not in a vital relationship with God so I can trust *Him*, then I will trust other people—pastors, bishops, theological professors, those with charisma, and those who make me feel good. I will always trust someone if I'm not trusting God. And if I'm not trusting God, I can just plan on it—sooner or later, I am going to be led astray.

Notice with me a well, and a woman who goes to that well during the middle of the day because she is not liked back in her home village of Sychar, in Samaria. She wasn't on the city council. She wasn't the director of the Girl Scouts program or the home and school. She was on the outs with the community because she'd had too many husbands, and the one she was living with at the time was not her husband. But it was an important meeting she attended at the well. It was one of those providential meetings, where she met Jesus, the Saviour of the world. You know about the conversation. The important thing is that her heart was touched. She accepted truth. Then she ran back to the town. She wasn't trying to hide anymore. "Come see a man who told me everything I ever did. Is not this the Christ, the Messiah?" (John 4:29, paraphrased).

If you check the story out, you will find something interesting: "Many of the Samaritans of that city believed on him for the saying of the woman, which testified, He told me all that ever I did" (verse 39). So, they chose *her* for their authority. Something spectacular had happened. It was in the realm of the supernatural, and we're all impressed by the spectacular. They decided that this woman must be someone they could rely on. They believed because of her. But the Bible goes on to say that "many more believed because of his [Jesus] own word" (verse 41). They came out to hear for themselves, and they "said unto the woman, Now we believe, not because of thy saying: for we have heard him ourselves, and know that this is indeed the Christ, the Saviour of the world" (verse 42).

That's where it's at. People too often fly by the seat of their britches (as the pilots say) in spiritual matters. It's all too common for people to become victims of spiritual vertigo in the religious realm. We often decide truth because it *feels* right or *feels* good rather than because it *is* right or *is* good.

The people of Angwin, California, will never forget the day a little light airplane took off from the Pacific Union College airport. It was foggy, but the travelers needed to make an appointment at Monterey Bay Academy. Unfortunately, an inexperienced pilot was at the controls, and he gave in to vertigo instead of trusting the instruments. The citizens of that community can still remember, and they are still haunted by the roar of the engine as it became louder and louder and finally buried itself in the ground along with the two passengers. They had been flying by the seat of their pants instead of by the proper instruments—the proper authority. They thought they were on the right track because it felt right.

I remember a time when I thought I was on the wrong track because it felt wrong, but it was right. My boy rushed into the house one day, all excited. He'd been to the beach with some student friends, who had taught him scuba diving. "Dad," he said, "you don't have to take classes and courses on scuba diving. There are just three or four rules you have to remember, that's all. You've got to go out with us next Sunday."

I wasn't sure about that. But I wanted to be a good dad,

and I remembered a missionary friend who came back from overseas and discovered that his son had taken up sky diving. My missionary friend went up and jumped out with him. I decided I would "go for it" with my son. Saturday night I practiced in the swimming pool in the backyard. It was easy there, with the tanks and the weights. The next day we went to the ocean. But instead of a clear day with blue sky and calm water and visibility forty feet deep, it was stormy and windy. The water was churned up with the sand, making it so a person could hardly see his hand in front of his face. Still, I swam out to the place where we were going to go down forty feet into the briny deep. But when I took a look through the murky waters, I said, "No thanks. I'm not going down." And I turned around and tried to swim for shore.

I had the tank and weights and something I could inflate to help me stay up, but I was taking on too much water to blow. I thrashed around, trying to make it to shore, but I had this illusion that I was going farther out to sea. I tried taking a breath of air from my tank, and I used up the whole tank in three gulps. I knew something was wrong! Finally, in a euphoric state, I gave up. I never thought of letting the weights go. After all, they were borrowed! I simply gave up in despair and decided to sink to the bottom. Just then, my knees touched the sand. I had been within walking distance for some time already. I had the *feeling* that I was on the wrong course, but I was actually on the right course all along.

The point is, don't fly by the seat of your britches and get vertigo going either direction. The devil will come along and say to you, as you struggle in the sea of life, "There is no chance for you. Some people are born to be fuel for the fires of hell, and you must be one of them. Go ahead and give up." But he's wrong. When you feel as if you're rejected and there's no hope for you, you will discover, at the very point of giving up, that the friendly shores of the heavenly country are beneath your feet.

That's good news, isn't it? Let's go by what Jesus tells us: "Whoever comes to me I will in no wise cast out"; "Come unto me . . . and I will give you rest" (John 6:37; Matthew 11:28). He is the same One who talked to the woman at the well. He is still speaking to us today, and He is our authority. He must be our only authority. Do you agree?

I have one short postscript to add to this chapter: Please, please, don't believe anything I said unless you check it out for yourself first.

Prostesting the Protestants

Chapter 3

Prostesting the Protestants

A man was once asked what he believed, and he said, "I believe what my church believes." Then they asked what his church believed, and he said, "The church believes what I believe." "Well," they said, "What is it that you both believe?" And he said, "We both believe the same thing."

If you are able to get from someone what they believe, there is a second question that almost always finishes them off: *Why* do you believe that? I have tried it out on people again and again. I have tried it out on Mormon missionaries who come to my door and on Jehovah's Witnesses. I have tried it out on my fellow church members. I have tried it out on the man in the street. And people have tried it out on me. Like the barber who asked me why I was a Seventh-day Adventist, and I thought I gave him a good Bible study. When I finished he said, "What was your father?"

"Well, he was a Seventh-day Adventist."

"And why are you a preacher?"

I thought I gave him a good answer, but he said, "What was your father?"

"Well, he was a preacher."

We *inherit* so many of our beliefs. We take them over from our parents and from our teachers. We get involved in a culture that convinces us of what we believe. So often, though, people become suddenly quiet when they're asked *why*. Sometimes, the only answer they can give is, "I always believed this way."

We are trying to take a look at the question of authority. Why do you believe, and why do you do what you do? In the previous chapter we noticed that it is the tendency of people everywhere—not only in the realm of religion, but in many areas—to be people centered. They depend on people. In the previous chapter I tried to make a strong case for *not* depending on people when it comes to truth and when it comes to things concerning our own destiny.

At the close of a sermon one week I made a plea not to believe anything I had said. Later I got this note: "If we are not supposed to believe anything we hear from the pulpit, then we also aren't supposed to believe that you just said, 'Don't believe what I said.' Therefore, shouldn't we believe what you said?"

I don't mean to be confusing, but I would like to challenge my own heart, along with anyone who reads this book, that we each make sure why we believe what we believe.

Today, in North America, most religious people are either Catholic, Protestant, or Jewish. Usually, when people are asked on quiz shows and questionnaires and job interviews about their religious persuasion, they find themselves under one of these three categories. And if you say you are a Protestant, the next question is: What are you protesting? Because a Protestant is one who protests something—a "protest-ant." This word actually came from the Diet of Spires in 1529 in Germany, where the famous "protest of the princes" became history. Under the leadership of Martin Luther, the monk who nailed his ninety-five theses to the church door, there arose a cloud of protestations against the religious system of that day. So please make sure what you're protesting if you are a Protestant.

If you were to go to the dictionary and find out what a

Protestant is, it would define it this way: "Any Christian not belonging to the Roman Catholic or Eastern Orthodox Church" *(Webster's New World Dictionary, Third College Edition)*. Some people feel that the Protestants are protesting primarily the Roman Catholic Church. But if we do that, we easily become divisive. So instead of trying to divide Protestants and Catholics more than they already are, I would like to suggest that we protest anything that is not supported by God's Word. That's what it was all about in the days of the protest of the princes in Germany.

The major elements of the Protestant reformation had to do with three things: (1) Justification by faith instead of by works; (2) everyone his own pope; and (3) *sola Scriptura*— the Bible only as our basis for authority. These were the three major truths of the Protestant reformation.

So, let's take a look at what makes a Protestant, without focusing unnecessarily on Roman Catholics. (I hope that anyone, whether Protestant, Catholic, or Jewish, who considers what we refer to here, would find it reasonable to join in protesting this way.)

The protest of the princes said, "We protest using anything other than the Word of God as our authority for doctrine and practice." This led the Roman Catholic Church to call the Council of Trent, which lasted for years and years and years. The bishops debated back and forth what they were going to do with this protest. As you know, the Catholic system of that time had two sources of authority: Scripture, which was chained to convent and monastery walls; and tradition, or beliefs handed down by the fathers of the church. And when it came to decide whether the Word of God or tradition would reign supreme, the Catholic Church said that tradition was above Scripture.

Martin Luther resisted this. The princes at the Diet of Spires resisted it. The whole Protestant reformation resisted it and came up instead with the conclusion that the

Bible must be our only rule, our only authority, for faith and practice. But in the Council of Trent, the Catholic Church reaffirmed its traditional position that the practices and traditions of the church handed down from the fathers still took precedence over Scripture.

Interestingly enough, in the process of time we came to another great Catholic Church council. It was called Vatican II. The church almost took the position at that assembly that Scripture is above tradition. But this resolution didn't quite make it. So the Catholic Church of today still teaches that the traditions of the church are above Scripture. This is one of the major issues separating Catholics and Protestants. However, there are many many Catholics today who have taken a long look at Scripture and are being encouraged by their leadership to study and understand the Bible. They are challenging their own church's teaching about tradition versus the Bible.

Jesus had something significant to say about authority: "Ye hypocrites, well did Esaias prophesy of you, saying, This people draweth nigh unto me with their mouth, and honoureth me with their lips; but their heart is far from me. But in vain they do worship me, *teaching for doctrines the commandments of men*" (Matthew 15:7-9, emphasis supplied). The religious system of His day was heavily into tradition, and they often put tradition ahead of Scripture. In fact, they multiplied their traditions.

Unfortunately, the Christian church today, including my own subculture, is not free from its enslavement to tradition. I would like to invite you to make a list sometime of some of the things you believe for which you can find no support in the Word of God, but that are simply the traditions of your church.

I can remember growing up thinking what a terrible thing it would be to open my eyes during prayer. I tried it a time or two and felt terribly guilty and smitten. In fact,

I can remember asking God to forgive me for this "sin"! Do you know of anything in God's Word on that point? It was a tradition, and still is. The question is, is it worthwhile? It's often worthwhile to shut out the distractions. But you certainly can't make a Bible-based practice out of that.

My wife and I were talking once to some people who, when they get into their cars to go on a trip, bow their heads and ask for God's care and protection as they go on their way. Is that a nice thing to do? Of course it is! Our friends asked us, "Do you do that?"

We said, "No, we don't."

"You don't!"

"No, we try to keep prayed up to date at other times."

What about putting something on top of the Bible, like another book? I can remember thinking what a terrible sin that would be. I still feel uncomfortable putting another book on top of the Bible. I think it's a nice tradition. But it is just a tradition. Make a list sometime of the things that Adventists do that have no real foundation in Scripture. You will find a number of little items.

But what about the big ones? Jesus said if we teach for doctrines the commandments of men, we worship Him . . . How? In vain!

This question of the Bible as authority led to a real problem in the time of Luther and the years that followed. The Catholic Church countered with the warning, "You cannot give the Bible to the common people. They won't know what to do with it. You'd better leave it chained to the monastery walls. You'd better let the church interpret it, because everybody will interpret it differently. It isn't safe to give the Bible into the hands of ordinary people."

Good question. Good challenge! What was the answer of the princes during their protest in Germany? They said, "This Holy Book is, in all things necessary for the Christian, easy of understanding, and calculated to scatter the darkness" (*The Great Controversy*, p. 203). And, if there are problems, "the Holy Scriptures ought to be explained by other and clearer texts" (ibid.).

This was another principle of the Protestant reformation. How has your church related to this question? When you read something in your Bible that is hard to understand, do you say, "Well, I'd better go ask the preacher or the priest or the prophet what that means"? Or do you say, "I am a simple layman, but I am armed with Scripture, and I can find the answer by searching in the same book." This was the premise of the Protestant reformers.

This was the approach to Scripture of a well-known preacher in the middle of the last century. His name was William Miller. He caused quite a stir among religious people of his day. He decided, as a Baptist farmer, that he was going to study the Bible for himself. So, he began to study with a concordance at his side. Whenever he came across a text that was hard to understand, he used the concordance to look up every other text he could find with the same wording or the same thought. In this way he let Scripture interpret Scripture. This was simply a reflection of the Protestant position since the days of the Reformation. Have you tried it?

Do we have helps today that give us the aid we really need to interpret Scripture with Scripture? *Strong's Exhaustive Concordance* and *Young's Concordance* are a tremendous help. You can open up Strong's or Young's concordance today and find every time the word *and* is used in Scripture! You can do a word study on *and*. I'm not sure why the compilers of these concordances included that word. I haven't really wanted to preach a sermon on *and* lately. But they were so comprehensive and so exhaustive that they insisted on including *every* word in *every* text that shows up in Scripture.

Then came the computer age. Someone helped me get

a Bible program in which I can push a button and my computer reads the entire Bible in three seconds and immediately shows me every time a particular word or phrase shows up! We have helps today that would make the pioneers' heads swim. It is possible for a simple layperson, armed with the computer, to do an exhaustive study of Scripture and find every verse that has to do with a particular topic, subject, or word, and in the process let Scripture interpret itself.

Seventh-day Adventists have taken a doctrinal position that is different from what most Christians believe. It has to do with what happens to us when we die. Why do we take the position that we are asleep in the grave, unconscious, until the resurrection? Why do we not believe people go to heaven or hell at death? Because early in our history, we insisted on following the historical Protestant position of taking every text in the Bible on the subject of death and what happens to us when we die and basing our teaching on the weight of evidence. At that point, if a few scriptures seem not to fit into that overall conclusion (like the rich man and Lazarus or the thief on the cross), we search for a better explanation of these passages. That is an example of the historic Protestant approach to Scripture.

So the Protestants said, "You don't have to have the prophet or the priest or the pope to interpret Scripture. A layperson can do it, and the Scriptures are easy to understand." But right there they made a big mistake. Because for the person who has not been born again, the Scriptures are not easy to understand. That's the one exception that we ought to make clear. Perhaps they assumed, when they made that statement, that everyone listening to what they said was already born again and spiritually in tune with the words of Scripture.

Notice the following passage of Scripture:

Now we have received, not the spirit of the world,
but the spirit which is of God; that we might know the
things that are freely given to us of God. Which things
also we speak, not in the words which man's wisdom
teacheth, but which the Holy Ghost teacheth; com-
paring spiritual things with spiritual (1 Corinthians
2:12).

That is an important principle of Bible interpretation.
However, there is an exception in verse 14: "The natural
man receiveth not the things of the Spirit of God: for they
are foolishness unto him: neither can he know them,
because they are spiritually discerned." Apart from the
miracle of the Holy Spirit in the life, the miracle of regen-
eration and of the new birth, the Scriptures are not easy to
understand, because they have to be looked at through
born-again spiritual glasses.

Another point of protest from the Reformation is that in
matters of faith, the majority has no power. This still rings
from the protest of the princes at the Diet of Spires. Are you
aware that the majority in the history of the religious world
has nearly, if not always, been wrong? Don't ever go by
what the majority decides. In this world the majority has
usually been wrong. So if you find the majority overwhelmingly agreeing on a particular point, the first thing to do is
to suspect it and then study it out for yourself. It is
dangerous to follow what the crowd does. It is dangerous to
follow what the majority do.

I remember reading an advertisement when I was a
teenager that said, "Acme Beer: Everyone is drinking it."
And they had pictures of different people drinking Acme
beer. The idea was that everybody is doing it, so you'd
better do it too. If everybody jumped off the Brooklyn
Bridge, you'd better do it too. What a sick argument!
Advertising and the media assume that the public is

gullible, and they treat people as if they were a thundering herd, rushing over the cliff. "Everybody is doing it; why don't you?" This is a dangerous argument, especially when it comes to religious issues. The Bible says, "Study to show thyself approved unto God, a workman that needeth not to be ashamed, rightly dividing the word of truth" (2 Timothy 2:15).

One principle that isn't simply Protestant is that prayer is the better part of study. It isn't safe to study the Bible without prayer. Study the example of Jesus. Study the example of the great people of the Bible and great people in the history of the Christian church. Martin Luther, when he faced some of his biggest crises, prayed three hours a day. In fact, he once said that any time his day was so busy that he didn't know how he would get everything done, he would make sure to take more time to pray. The question with him was not, Do I have time to pray? It was, Do I have time *not* to pray? That was his position, and that has been the position of people ever since who follow in the wake of the Protestant reformation.

I would like to add another principle to the study of God's Word and prayer: Christian service and witness, or outreach. All three of these go together to make the Bible meaningful and understandable. Because then we have a reason to search, the power to search with, and the spiritual insight without which we're dead.

Another great principle of the Protestant reformation is justification by faith. The infamous Tetzel had gone out beating his drum, trying to get people to buy indulgences. When he got to Germany, he found that someone had been softening up the people for deeper things. Luther said, "I will poke a hole in Tetzel's drum." Tetzel tried to get the people to pay money so that when they died, or when their relatives died, their souls, instead of languishing in purgatory, would rise to heaven. Of course, the whole thing was based on the false principle of the merit system—that a person can earn or pay for God's favor. Luther was vehemently opposed to this.

Justification by faith teaches that our standing and our eternal destiny with God are not based on what we do. They are based on what Jesus has done. A Christian is a Christian because of whom he knows. Salvation depends on the righteousness of Jesus, never on our own righteousness. A Christian never goes to heaven because of anything he has done, and he's never lost because of anything he does. The only reason we are saved or lost is because of how we relate to Jesus. This was the bombshell that shook the dominant religious institution to its foundations in the days of the Reformation.

A protestant, whether Catholic, Jew, or Protestant, is anyone who protests any system that teaches that we can in any way save ourselves by what we do. Is that part of your protesting? Have you thought about it lately?

The Protestants in the days of the Reformation were known for their courage. I mean, we could go through story after story and quotation after quotation from those days. They knew how to fight a good fight. They would defend truth with their lives, and that's why millions of martyrs gave their lives for the cause of truth during the Dark Ages. Listen to these ringing words from those courageous people.

Tyndale said, "I defy the Pope and all his laws. And if God spares my life ere many years, I will cause a boy that driveth the plow to know more of the scriptures than you do." Those were words to get burned by!

Listen to Luther in his debate with John Eck at the Diet of Worms: "A simple layman armed with Scripture is greater than the greatest pope without it."

When Luther said that, John Eck jumped to his feet and shouted, "Heresy, Martin Luther, heresy."

Whereupon Luther shouted back, "Heresy? So be it! It is *still* the truth." Then he said, "You may expect everything from me except flight and recantation. Fly I cannot, and still less retract." And in his famous speech when he was called before the prelates he said, "Here I stand, I can do no other, so help me God."

Is my purpose today in talking about Protestants to make the pope look bad? No. The truth is, I like today's pope. But in the days when darkness was so deep that people were not thinking for themselves, but only believed what was told them, these principles came out. They should be the principles today of everyone, whether Catholic, Protestant, or Jew.

So, in conclusion, I would like to protest the Protestants. I am protesting those Protestants who have forgotten that the Bible is the basis of their authority. I am protesting the Protestants who have forgotten that the Bible interprets itself and needs no interpreter. I am protesting the Protestants who have forgotten that the majority is not usually right. It is usually wrong, and it has no power. I am protesting the Protestants who have forgotten the significance of prayer as the basis of meaningful study. I am protesting the Protestants who have so long taken for granted that we are saved only by God's grace and not by our own works that they seldom talk about it. And I am protesting the Protestants who become wimps in the presence of anything that would threaten their Protestant stand.

In the process of protesting the Protestants, I am protesting myself. Who am I to stand up and be a shining example? But I do know what I would like to be by God's grace. Do you? Are you a Protestant? Are you really? Do you know what you are protesting in the process? May we pray that God makes us certain of our authority and why we believe what we believe.

Jesus and the Prophets

Chapter 4

Jesus and the Prophets

*T*here was a college Sabbath School class on a campus where I was pastoring. A group of students had been given a list of questions about the lesson for that week, and a leader had been appointed to lead the discussion. The subject of the lesson was predestination.

As the first question was being discussed, one of the students said, "My ninth-grade teacher said this on the subject."

And the group leader said, "That's a good thought, thank you."

As the lesson continued, a second person spoke. "I think that . . . ," and she gave her own opinion of the answer to the question.

The group leader said, "That was very helpful. I'd never thought of it that way before."

A third student said, "In our Sabbath School lesson quarterly, one of our church leaders is quoted as saying such and such."

The leader said enthusiastically, "That's a terrific idea."

Finally a fourth person ventured to quote a sentence from the book *The Story of Redemption.* At that point the leader frowned and said, "I think we should stick to the Bible and the Bible only."

This happened to be near the beginning of a time when this whole topic of spiritual gifts began to come into focus in the Adventist Church. And, as you know, there has been a lot of dialogue since. In fact, there has been so much dialogue that I am a little nervous to even bring up the subject. I have tried to find a way out of addressing this topic, but I cannot. So I am going to address it the best I know how, because it is something I personally believe in deeply. Yet I am painfully aware that many people have serious questions concerning spiritual gifts in the church.

In the Reformation days, you remember, they had these three great phrases that we've been noticing. Justification by faith, the priesthood of believers, and *sola Scriptura* (the Bible only). But the interesting thing is that *sola Scriptura* is not scriptural. You would have a hard time proving from Scripture the principle of *sola Scriptura*. Even Martin Luther said something rather interesting. He insisted on *sola Scriptura* unless there is clear further and tested revelation. And, if you go back in the history of authority for religious belief and thought, you immediately come face to face with the realization that for two and a half thousand years after Adam and Eve were created, there was no such thing as *Scriptura*. So, what did they go by? They went by the revelation of God through the prophets and through gifts that God had given to His church.

I have tried to prove *sola Scriptura* from Scripture, and I find it very difficult to do so. In fact, even the canon of Scripture is not scriptural! You're aware, no doubt, that many prophets wrote books during the time our Bible was being formed. Eventually, certain ones were included, and others were left out. But there is nothing in the Bible that tells how that happened. The amazing thing is that some of your best support for the Reformation principle of *sola Scriptura* comes from nonscriptural sources. In fact, one of the best supports for *sola Scriptura*, or the Bible and the

Bible only, as a basis for doctrine, faith, and practice, is found in a book called *The Great Controversy!* You may have read it. So if you're going to hold tightly to the principle of Scripture only as your base of authority, one of your best supports is from a nonscriptural source. Rather interesting, isn't it?

What was the meaning of the Reformation phrase, *sola Scriptura?* Did it mean there was no manifestation of light outside of Scripture? No. Not even Luther took that stand. What it meant was that we must have Scripture authority for doctrine and practice, not simply church tradition and teaching. And the Reformers made a strong appeal for that. However, people today have found it convenient to use *sola Scriptura* for other reasons—shall we call them lesser reasons, maybe even baser reasons? They use *sola Scriptura* to do away with spiritual gifts, or added revelation, because some people don't like these. One of the other phrases from the Reformation that has been turned into another use is "the priesthood of believers." In the days of the Reformation this meant that everyone has immediate access to God, and no one has to go through saints or priests. But today people are using the idea of the priesthood of believers as a motto against church organization and leadership, which was not what the Reformers had in mind at all.

Anyone who goes by the Bible and the Bible only has to accept spiritual gifts, because spiritual gifts are scriptural. In 1 Corinthians 12:1 Paul makes it clear that God does not want the church to lack any gift. Notice the description of these spiritual gifts in Ephesians: "When he [Jesus] ascended up on high, he led captivity captive, and gave gifts unto men." "And he gave some, apostles; and some, prophets; and some, evangelists; and some, pastors and teachers" (Ephesians 4:8, 11).

Most of us have seen apostles, because apostles were

those who were sent out. I grew up watching missionaries come home and tell stories from the mission field. In fact, my ambition was to be a "returned missionary." Most of us have seen some real-live evangelists, and we've all seen pastors and teachers. But most of us have never even come close to seeing a prophet. I "saw one" in the streets of New York near Times Square once. That was a scary experience. I think he was out of some state institution, and he was really letting the people have it with fire and brimstone. But to see a genuine prophet would be a unique experience.

Some people have modified the meaning of the word *prophet*. A prophet, they say, is one who speaks forth the Word of God, and that's it. By that definition any preacher could be a prophet. But in the Bible the word *prophet* included more than that. And some were called more than prophets, which is interesting too!

What did God have in mind when He gave us these gifts, including prophets? The Bible answers that question: "For the perfecting of the saints, for the work of the ministry, for the edifying of the body of Christ [the church]. Till we all come in the unity of the faith, and of the knowledge of the Son of God, unto a perfect man, unto the measure of the stature of the fullness of Christ" (Ephesians 4:12, 13). Notice particularly verse 14: "That we henceforth be no more children, tossed to and fro, and carried about with every wind of doctrine, by the sleight of men, and cunning craftiness, whereby they lie in wait to deceive; but speaking the truth in love, may grow up into him in all things, which is the head, even Christ." God had a real purpose for these gifts to the church—all five of them, including the gift of prophecy. And we certainly haven't come to the time fulfilling this prediction—the time when we no longer need these gifts. If we ever needed them before, we sure do need them now!

I have been painfully aware of how obscure the church's

mission and message are in the minds of many, many people. In fact, the Pacific Union Conference president, in his challenge speech during a recent constituency meeting, said, "There are three things that are tremendously crucial right now. Number one: What is our mission? Number two: Why don't we have more confidence in leadership? And number three: Our need for revival in the church."

If we ever needed all the gifts that God has to give, we need them today. Don't you think so?

So, spiritual gifts are biblical. And if you believe in *sola Scriptura*, then you believe in spiritual gifts. They are solidly Bible-based, including the gift of prophecy.

In the post-Reformation times, hundreds of voices began to tell what they thought the Bible meant, which resulted in the hundreds of denominations we have today. And the multiplication of groups continues, each one claiming to march under the banner of *sola Scriptura*. So what are we going to do with all the divergent views and different conclusions, all supposedly based on the same Scripture? Certainly Ephesians 4:14 is very meaningful here: "That we . . . be no more children, tossed to and fro . . . [by] every wind of doctrine." God had a specific purpose for giving us the gift called the gift of prophecy. He gave it to guide and unify the church. In the history of the Christian church, including the Old Testament, there were prophets available when the church was close to God; and when the church wasn't close to God, the voices of the prophets ceased. That's a very interesting trend! There were exceptions, when there was a lone voice, such as Elijah, calling the whole nation to repentance. But as far as the special gift of the prophets to God's people, there was a definite relationship between their closeness to God or their distance from God. Sometimes we say in the Adventist Church that we have the gift of prophecy. No, we don't. We *had* the gift. We *used* to have it. The gift of prophecy is a present-tense thing, not a past-tense thing. Think about that carefully. This is biblically true. So the absence of spiritual gifts—all of them—really says something to us about our need for revival.

What is the purpose of the gift of prophecy in general? Can we put it into a few words? One wonderful purpose has been to take varying interpretations of Scripture and help us understand which one is correct so we can understand the difference between truth and error. One person even called the Spirit of Prophecy "the referee." When someone has worked hard to study out truth from Scripture and someone else has worked hard to study out the truth from Scripture, and they don't agree, then God gives His stamp of approval through the prophet by saying, "This is it."

The prophetic gift is not for the purpose of introducing or initiating new truth. It is for the purpose of clarifying truth and making it easy to understand. It throws light on truth that is already there. So the purpose of the gifts in the church is for understanding, for confirmation, for clarification, for explanation, sometimes to warn, sometimes to enlighten, sometimes to comfort. It is God, trying all the time to bring help to the body of Christ, His church.

The prophets were lesser lights leading to the greater light. They were not the light that is the basis of authority. The prophets were not authorities *over* the Bible. They were authorities *on* the Bible.

In the days of Christ we have an interesting example of one of the greatest of the prophets, through which we can see how Jesus related to the prophets. Let's notice a tense moment in the life of Jesus. It was close to the time of His death. In fact, it was the night before His crucifixion. Jesus had been taken captive in the Garden of Gethsemane. He had been pushed and shoved from Caiaphas to Annas. He'd gone to Pilate, and Pilate sent Him to Herod. "And when Herod saw Jesus, he was exceeding glad: for he was desirous to see him of a long season, because he had heard many things of him; and he hoped to have seen some miracle done by him. Then he questioned with him in many words; but he [Jesus] answered him nothing" (Luke 23:8, 9).

Have you ever gotten the silent treatment? How does it feel? Jesus "answered him nothing." Who was this Herod? He was the one who had silenced the voice of John the Baptist. Jesus said concerning John the Baptist, "Of those born of women, there was never one greater" (Matthew 11:11, paraphrased). Yet Herod, because of a drunken party and a rash promise, had John the Baptist beheaded. So when I read how Jesus stood before Herod and answered him not a word, I said, "Good! That serves him right. Let him have it, Lord. Look at him with daggers. Have a scowl on Your face. Grind Your teeth. But don't say anything to him. Give him the silent treatment. He deserves it." That's the way I would have done it.

But Jesus came to die for Herod as much as for anyone else. So instead of the scenario that I tend to fantasize, we'd better take a look at the tears in Jesus' eyes and the lump in His throat, as He realized that here was one more of those who had been created to live forever, but had turned down the offer. By His silence Jesus was saying to Herod, "You ignored the voice of My prophet, and there is nothing more I can do for you. You made your decision concerning the prophet, and I can't help you. Because you silenced the voice of the gift of prophecy, there is nothing more." Jesus didn't give Herod the silent treatment because He was trying to insult him or be rude. It was pointless to say more.

John the Baptist was *more* than a prophet. This has happened at least twice in the history of biblical personalities. In Matthew 11:9, Jesus said that John the Baptist was more than a prophet, and in verse 10 He called John His messenger, the Lord's messenger. He also made it clear that John the Baptist was the fulfillment of "Elijah, the prophet that was to come" (verse 14). At the close of the Old Testament, in Malachi, the prediction was made that before the great and terrible day of the Lord, Elijah would come back (see Malachi 4:5). John the Baptist was a partial fulfillment of this. But according to Malachi, at the very end of time, just before Jesus comes, that prophecy is to be fulfilled in its fullness. So, if you ever hear of anyone who is more than a prophet and who is called the Lord's messenger and who is a lesser light to lead people to the greater light, you need to take careful heed and pay special attention.

John the Baptist was a lesser light. Matthew 3:13, 14 says that when Jesus came to be baptized in the Jordan River, John said, "I am not even worthy to tie your shoe-strings. I have need to be baptized of you." Later, as Jesus' popularity began to grow and John's began to decrease, John said, "He must increase, but I must decrease" (John 3:30). John the Baptist, the fulfillment of Elijah—Elijah the second—was a lesser light to lead people to the greater light.

Let's go back to the Old Testament record, where we have the other Bible personality who was more than a prophet.

And Miriam and Aaron spake against Moses, . . . and they said, Hath the Lord indeed spoken only by Moses? hath he not spoken also by us? And the Lord heard it. Now the man Moses was very meek, above all the men which were upon the face of the earth.

And the Lord spake suddenly unto Moses, and unto Aaron, and unto Miriam, Come out ye three unto the tabernacle of the congregation. And they three came out. And the Lord came down in the pillar of the cloud, and stood in the door of the tabernacle, and called

Aaron and Miriam: and they both came forth. And he said, Hear now my words: If there be a prophet among you, I the Lord will make myself known unto him in a vision, and will speak unto him in a dream. My servant Moses is not so, who is faithful in all mine house. With him will I speak mouth to mouth. [Apparently God considered Moses more than a prophet.]

And then God said to Miriam and Aaron,

Wherefore then were ye not afraid to speak against my servant Moses? And the anger of the Lord was kindled against them; and he departed. And the cloud departed from off the tabernacle; and, behold, Miriam became leprous, white as snow: and Aaron looked upon Miriam, and, behold, she was leprous.

And Aaron said unto Moses, Alas, my lord, I beseech thee, lay not the sin upon us, wherein we have done foolishly, and wherein we have sinned. Let her not be as one dead. . . . And Moses cried unto the Lord, saying, Heal her now, O God, I beseech thee.

And the Lord said unto Moses, If her father had but spit in her face, should she not be ashamed seven days? Let her be shut out from the camp seven days, and after that let her be received in again. And Miriam was shut out from the camp seven days: and the people journeyed not till Miriam was brought in again.

That was a tense moment in the Old Testament record, which happened as a result of what? Someone who was not afraid to speak against God's servant. It was serious business, in the days of the prophets and those who were more than prophets, to speak against them, let alone put them to death, as Herod did. No wonder Jesus stood in utter helplessness in the presence of Herod. When Herod silenced the prophet, he also silenced Jesus. There was nothing more Jesus could say.

This brings us to a major conclusion for today: Anyone who is unfriendly to the prophets sooner or later is going to be unfriendly to Jesus. That is a given. It is an axiom. It is a biblical principle that the way you treat the prophets is the way you will treat Jesus.

Now the religious people in Christ's day had some real problems. Jesus called them hypocrites. He said it plainly: "Wherefore ye be witnesses unto yourselves, that ye are the children of them which killed the prophets. Fill ye up then the measure of your fathers. Ye serpents, ye generation of vipers, how can ye escape the damnation of hell?" (Matthew 23:31-33). Hard-hitting words by Jesus, who had tears in His voice when He said them.

In Acts 7 we have the record of Stephen, who we say was the first Christian martyr. I don't think so. I think John the Baptist was the first Christian martyr—or perhaps it was Abel. But Stephen was the first Christian martyr in the early Christian church. And as he stood defending Jesus, he noticed the scowls on the people's faces. Finally, he broke from his sermon and said, "Which of the prophets have not your fathers persecuted?" (Acts 7:52). It was at this point that they gnashed at him with their teeth and took him out and stoned him.

In Luke 16 Jesus told the story of the rich man and Lazarus. The rich man was pleading for someone to tell his brothers about what happened to him, but Jesus said, "If they hear not Moses and the prophets, neither will they be persuaded, though one rose from the dead" (Luke 16:31). Again we see the biblical principle that if we turn our backs on the gift of prophecy, there is nothing more God can do.

Jesus had a healthy respect for the prophets. In Matthew 5:17 He said, "I came not to destroy the law or the prophets" (paraphrased). In Luke we have the record of Jesus coming to His hometown and reading from the prophet Isaiah, and He said, "This day is this scripture fulfilled in your ears" (Luke 4:21). And they took Him out and tried to throw Him off the cliff after church. Jesus quoted from all the prophets, including Daniel, Jonah, and Moses. As Jesus wept over Jerusalem, He said, "O Jerusalem, Jerusalem, thou that killest the prophets, and stonest them which are sent unto thee" (Matthew 23:37). Jesus always had a high regard for the gift of prophecy, and He defended it strongly.

On the morning of the resurrection, Jesus walked with two companions. He reasoned with them from Moses and *all* the prophets, concerning Himself (see Luke 24:27). Again, in Matthew 15, He warned the people against teaching for doctrine the commandments of men (see Matthew 15:9). As He spoke plainly to them, the disciples came and said, "Lord, don't You know that they were offended?"

Jesus said, "Leave them alone. They're blind." And then He told one of His shortest parables. "If the blind try to lead the blind, they're all going to fall into the ditch" (see Matthew 15:12-14). What was their problem? The people had lost their vision. They had lost their eyesight. Do you remember that 1 Corinthians likens the church to the body, and it talks about the eyes (12:16, 17)? This reminds me of one of the names for a prophet in the Old Testament. They were called "seers" (see, for example, 1 Samuel 9:9). I used to wonder, when I was a child, what the word *seers* meant. I didn't realize it was talking about the eyes of the church—the see-ers. It is through the gift of prophecy that God helps people to "see" the issues of life more clearly. And when the people in Christ's day demonstrated their blindness, they were simply acknowledging, in spite of themselves, that they had turned from the prophets, or the gift of prophecy.

I am not mentioning any names here, on purpose. I am just saying to those who know their Bibles that, if you're going to believe what the Bible says concerning all the gifts that God has for His church, then you have to believe in the gift of prophecy. It's just that simple. Which means that *sola Scriptura* is not scriptural, because *sola Scriptura* guides you to the prophets. And the amazing thing is that the prophets, if they are real, guide you back to Scripture!

The story is told of a man who went to a gallery of famous artwork. As he was viewing the paintings, he remarked to his companion, "They say this stuff sells for millions of dollars. Why, I wouldn't give you a nickel for the whole lot of it."

A guard was standing nearby. Hearing the man's comments, he stepped over to him, tapped him on the shoulder, and said, "Sir, these paintings are not on trial. But those who view them are."

Maybe that's not too far off. You may think that the gift of prophecy is on trial, but it is you and I who are on trial, in how we relate to God's authority.

We could spend many more chapters on this. I'm going to spare you for now. But as we consider our basis for what we believe and *why* we do what we do, let's make sure not to leave out one of the greatest gifts that the church has ever had. And remember, in conclusion, that they way you treat the prophets is the way you will treat Jesus in the end. That's how it is.

Wonderful Counselor

Chapter 5

Wonderful Counselor

Where do you go when you need counsel? Where do you go when you need a counselor? Today it's almost in vogue to be "in therapy" or to be going to a counselor.

And what kind of counsel do you give when someone wants *you* to hang up *your* shingle? After a few years of watching this scene, I have developed some thoughts about God's plan for counseling. And shouldn't we understand the crucial difference between Christian counseling and non-Christian counseling?

I'd like to begin by setting forth some principles for getting counsel. The first principle is that God should be our first and most important counselor.

The Bible speaks about someone who is a Wonderful Counselor. We hear this verse at least once a year at Christmastime: "For unto us a child is born, unto us a son is given: and the government shall be upon his shoulder: and his name shall be called Wonderful, Counsellor, The mighty God, The everlasting Father, The Prince of Peace" (Isaiah 9:6). Those are interesting names, all used in addressing Jesus. The King James Version puts a comma between "wonderful" and "counselor," but I'm going to remove the comma and call Him the Wonderful Counselor. That's how most of the newer versions say it.

If you're in need of a counselor, have you checked with the One the Bible says is the best Counselor of all? Are you one of His clients? Have you compared His prices?

He is the Wonderful Counselor because He is the Mighty God. In Romans the apostle Paul, overwhelmed with the reality of who God is, said, "O the depth of the riches both of the wisdom and knowledge of God! how unsearchable are his judgments, and his ways past finding out. For who hath known the mind of the Lord? or *who hath been his counselor?*" (Romans 11:33, emphasis supplied). When you finally come to the One who made us, who knows what makes us tick, you realize that He's the One who doesn't need a counselor. He's the One who is the Wonderful Counselor.

I've checked into some of the inspired information we have been given about this field. Here's a sample:

> Some [people] are weak in Christian experience because . . . [they] have sought for the approval of man with far greater anxiety than for the approval of God. They have looked to mankind for help and counsel more than to God. . . . And too often those of whom they sought counsel needed help themselves; for their souls were not right with God. . . . Trust in the wisdom of man does not facilitate growth in grace" (*Gospel Workers*, p. 414).

That's a hard-hitting comment coming from the days of our church's founders. "Trust in the wisdom of man does not facilitate growth in grace."

Most of us are aware that we are going to depend on someone. We have the privilege of depending on God, but if we choose not to depend on Him, we're going to depend on people. And there we have two choices: We will either depend on ourselves, or we will depend on others. If we have a low self-image and are not self-sufficient, we will choose to depend on others and seek their approval.

Sin began with self-sufficiency. In fact, pride and self-sufficiency are the most hopeless sins. We're not talking here about self-worth. Not at all. We understand that God is disappointed when we place a low estimate on ourselves. The Bible truth is that we are helpless to produce righteousness, and we're really helpless to do anything apart from God. But just because we're helpless does not mean that we are worthless. We are worth everything in the eyes of heaven, and God wants us to place a high estimate on ourselves. But if I choose not to depend on God, the way Lucifer did in the beginning, then I'm likely to depend on myself and become self-sufficient.

Does this mean that we should always seek God's advice alone and never seek counsel from another human being? Of course not! The Bible says that a wise man listens to counsel, and plans fail for lack of counsel, but with many advisers they succeed (see Proverbs 12:15; 15:22).

So when we need human counsel, to whom should we turn? Let's look at the very first verse of the first psalm. It's talking about a blessing in store for someone in particular: "Blessed is the man [or woman] that walketh not in the counsel of the ungodly, nor standeth in the way of sinners, nor sitteth in the seat of the scornful." That's rather pointed, isn't it? "Blessed is the one who does not walk in the counsel of the *ungodly*."

Here is another sample from some of our own writings of the past: "Jesus said, 'Beware of men' [beware of mankind]. They [the disciples] were not to put implicit confidence in those who knew not God. . . . God is dishonored and the gospel is betrayed when His servants depend on the counsel of men who are not under the guidance of the Holy Spirit. Worldly wisdom is foolishness with God. Those who rely upon it will surely err" (*The Desire of Ages*, p. 354).

Do not put confidence in those who know not God!

Many people in the counseling field today are actually trained *not* to bring in God because they don't want to be, as one person put it, "so heavenly minded that they are no earthly good." So they leave God out of the picture.

So what should we do when we need counsel for a marital problem or an emotional problem? We should seek the help of a Christian who is professionally trained to deal with such problems. The question is, What is a Christian?

"Well, a Christian doctor is one who goes to church," you say.

Not necessarily. There are all kinds of bad reasons for going to church.

"A Christian is one who believes in God," you say.

Not necessarily.

"A Christian doctor is one who believes the Bible is God's Word."

Again, not necessarily.

A Christian doctor or psychiatrist or counselor is one who went through Loma Linda University.

Not necessarily.

So what is a Christian doctor, preacher, or teacher?

Most people define a Christian in terms of behavior and morality, and they scarcely mention the name of Jesus. But as I understand it, the Christian is one who loves to think and talk about Jesus. Christ is the center of his or her focus. I have talked with counselors a few times, and it was a wonderful thing to have them bring Jesus into the center of the discussion. Some people can't handle that. They won't stand for it.

There are good counselors and bad counselors. A bad counselor might have a Ph.D. and all the training that goes with it, but simply capitalize on people's need to depend on someone. A bad therapist will encourage patients to depend on him just as long as he can. After all, that way he makes more money.

The better therapist is the one who allows the client to depend on him only as long as it takes to get the client back to depending on himself again. But the essence of Jesus' teaching was self-surrender—the need to depend on God.

A good Christian counselor will allow the client to depend on him only as long as it takes to lead his client to depend on God. And, in the process, the Christian counselor will not hesitate, when the time is right, to talk about Jesus and help the person think about Jesus, the Wonderful Counselor. If you know of any counselors like that who are also professionals in their field, let it be known! We need all of these people we can get.

The Bible makes it very clear that anyone who trusts in his own heart is a fool. So if I'm a counselor who is trying to get someone to become self-sufficient and self-contained, I am teaching that person to be a fool. If that's the best the client will allow me to do, then of course leaving God out of the picture is their choice. And it's also their biggest problem.

But the Christian counselor will point people to the Wonderful Counselor. He realizes how inadequate it is, and how temporary it is, to depend on a therapist. The Bible says, "Put not your trust in princes, nor in the son of man in whom there is no help. His breath goeth forth, he returneth to his earth; in that very day his thoughts perish" (Psalm 146:3, 4).

So what is a Christian counselor? What kind of counselor should you and I look for when we need therapy? It should be one who will not allow me to escape from God or even provide me with a professional way to escape from God. A Christian counselor will get me in touch with God as fast as possible.

I believe that many ordinary people—neighbors,

friends, and relatives—could do a lot more than therapists often do in terms of teaching people to depend on the Wonderful Counselor. This has become extremely crucial today because apparently there are those who are misusing their profession.

As I look at the different methods of counseling used today, I find myself wondering, "What approach did Jesus use when He counseled people? Was He a Wonderful Counselor indeed?"

We find that Jesus used both the direct and nondirect approach to counseling. He was a master at both. Apparently He knew when to use the direct and when to use the nondirect methods. The Bible gives several examples of the direct method. For instance, a man came to Jesus one night. His name was Nicodemus. And he said to Jesus, "I would like to have an intellectual discussion with someone, and You look like a good candidate."

But Jesus said, "What you need is to be born again."

That would be the direct approach to counseling.

What about the Samaritan woman, with whom Jesus started out with the nondirective method. "Could I have a glass of water?" And pretty soon He said, "Go call your husband; you have five of them, and the one you're with now is not one" (see John 4:7, 16-18). That would be the direct approach, wouldn't it?

Then there are the scribes and Pharisees who came to Jesus one time and said, "What about our descent from Abraham. We put a lot of stock in our forefathers" (see John 8:33, 44). And Jesus said, "Abraham is not your father. You are of your father the devil." That sounds direct as well.

On another occasion a Syrophoenician woman came to Jesus because her daughter was grievously vexed with a demon. Jesus first of all answered her not a word. I don't know if you call that indirect, but pretty soon He said to her, "It's not right to take the children's food and cast it to dogs."

That's rather direct (see Matthew 15:26). But He knew the kind of material He was working with. The ultimate moment came when she said, "Truth, Lord: Yet the dogs eat of the crumbs which fall from their masters' table" (verse 27).

Maybe you've heard about the Pharisees who invited Jesus over for dinner and then complained about the way His disciples washed their hands. Jesus said, "You fools" (Luke 11:40). That's a direct approach.

Jesus was also very skilled at the indirect method of dealing with people. For example, when He was twelve years old, He went into a nondirective session with certain doctors of the law in the temple, and He began to ask them questions. We're told that if they had followed through on the insights that were triggered by these questions, there would have been a religious awakening like the world had never seen. But they refused. They did not want the Wonderful Counselor from above. They thought they were teaching Him. But He, for a time, was teaching them.

Look at the rich young ruler who came to Jesus and said, "What good thing shall I do?" And Jesus indirectly led him around to where He had him examine his own heart. Then it became clear what his real problem was. And he went away sorrowful.

An excellent example of the indirect approach happened during a feast at the home of a Pharisee named Simon. Simon had led Mary into sin, and then of all things, Jesus healed him in his wretched Pharisaical condition. So he tried to pay Jesus back by inviting him to dinner. After dinner Mary came and anointed Jesus' feet, and Simon was critical. So Jesus asked a simple question: "Which one is going to love the most, the one who is forgiven the most or the one who is forgiven the least?" (see Luke 7:40-42). No one else knew what He was getting at, but Simon got the message. That was an indirect approach that won his heart. Jesus shielded him from embarrassment in the presence of his friends.

Look at the walk to Emmaus where the two disciples who were with Jesus later said, "Did not our heart burn within us?" (Luke 24:32). They didn't even know who He was as He asked them questions and reasoned with them concerning the Scriptures.

Then you have Jesus before Herod, the one who had put John the Baptist to death. And it says, "He answered him nothing" (Luke 23:9). That would be rather nondirect, wouldn't it? But that was the only thing that could be done. He must have done it with tears as He faced another one of God's children who refused the Wonderful Counselor.

Where did Jesus get the wisdom to know how to treat people, when to be direct and when to be nondirect? As I understand it, He got it from above Him, not from within Himself. He was 4,000 years downhill from Adam in mental power, but He knew how to keep in touch with the Wonderful Counselor above Him.

They tell us that catharsis is very important. I'm not sure of the technical definition, but apparently it has something to do with helping people let the dam go as the problems that have been piling up for years sort of flow out in the presence of someone who loves them. Jesus was a master of catharsis. The man was let down through the roof. He was a paralytic. But the thing he wanted most was the assurance that his sins were forgiven. And Jesus went so far as to call this victim of a social disease "Son!" And then He said, "Thy sins be forgiven thee" (Matthew 9:2). And the load left him. In the end, it was a package deal, because he was healed as well.

Think about the woman dragged to Jesus, and the first words she heard from Him, "I don't condemn you." "I don't condemn you. Go and sin no more" (see John 8:11). And that is possible only in the presence of someone who really doesn't condemn.

Look at Jesus kneeling down and washing the disciples' feet. One of the greatest awakenings came to them as they realized the difference between pride and humility. But they realized it in the presence of Someone who treated them tenderly and in love, who accepted them the way they were.

And then don't forget the thief on the cross, who found himself in the presence of Someone who loved everybody. He was constrained to say, "Lord, remember me in Your kingdom" (see Luke 23:42). Jesus was indeed a Wonderful Counselor!

Whenever you need a counselor—and that probably happens more than most of us realize—be sure you find a Christian counselor. And whenever you are asked to give counsel, even if you don't have a shingle or a degree beside your name, remember that a Christian counselor turns people to Jesus. That's the best you or anyone else can offer them. If they won't have that, then they will waste a lot of time and money, because worldly wisdom is only temporary and in the end will amount to nothing.

I would like to recommend to you the Wonderful Counselor. You are safe with Him. And what's more, He really loves you.

A wonderful Savior is Jesus my Lord,
A wonderful Savior to me,
He hideth my soul in the cleft of the rock,
Where rivers of pleasure I see.

He hideth my soul in the cleft of the rock
That shadows a dry, thirsty land;
He hideth my life in the depths of His love
And covers me there with His hand.

Spiritual
Schizophrenia

Chapter 6

Spiritual Schizophrenia

S piritual schizophrenia is a problem that most of us have struggled with, in spite of the fact that we usually think that these people live in the state hospital or similar places. This is a very practical topic, even though we run a risk in trying to address the question of psychiatry and counseling. But I think we're safe as long as we try to stay with what the Bible has to tell us.

Our text is Matthew 23. We will spend some time looking at this chapter. Let's look first at the nature of the disease as Jesus described it in verses 25 to 28. Jesus was talking to the religious leaders of His day. He said,

> Woe unto you, scribes and Pharisees, hypocrites! for ye make clean the outside of the cup and of the platter, but within they are full of extortion and excess. Thou blind Pharisee, cleanse first that which is within the cup and platter, that the outside of them may be clean also. Woe unto you, scribes and Pharisees, hypocrites! for ye are like unto whited sepulchres, which indeed appear beautiful outward, but are within full of dead men's bones, and of all uncleanness. Even so ye also outwardly appear righteous unto men, but within ye are full of hypocrisy and iniquity.

I guess it's obvious from this scripture that Jesus was talking about people who were one way on the outside and another way on the inside. Perhaps, for starters, we might call this the multiple personality.

I can remember going with a psychology class from La Sierra University over to the state hospital and listening to the doctors as they interviewed patients there. Before they brought each patient in, they told us what the problem was and what we could expect to happen when they triggered the "button" that set the patient off talking about the other person he thought he was. I felt sorry for these unfortunate people.

But I have thought a lot about this since. We see much the same thing in the church. People get triggered into quivering lips and tears and become someone else entirely. I have had my struggles with schizophrenia in the spiritual realm. One thing that brings me comfort is that most of you have too. Because we are a part of a church that is known at the end as Laodicea, and Laodicea is known for being lukewarm. I used to wonder how lukewarm (if we were going to follow the kitchen-sink model) someone could be who is hot on the left side and cold on the right side. But the Scripture interpretation of lukewarm is right here in Matthew 23. It's a person who is hot on the outside and cold on the inside. It's a person who goes through all the right motions, who wouldn't think of doing anything wrong. It's a person who cares nothing about God but still tries to be a good, law-abiding citizen and maintain a good reputation. Such a person is a victim of something called mere morality, which is worthwhile, but not religion, and not righteousness. We are born with this problem. According to Scripture, we are all born in sin, which means we are born separated from God. Self is the center of our focus. That is the first common denominator, and out of it all the rest of the thoughts and motives and purposes and secret intents of the heart arise. We learn by training, by culture, and by our own frame of reference how to control the outside. But Jesus had something much better to offer. He wants to change us so that we are the same on the inside as we are on the outside.

The problem of Laodicea is that they don't know their problem. That's often the case in the medical field. People are not aware when it comes to their pathological problems.

Let's take a look at the diagnosis in Matthew 23. We are going to be spiritual psychiatrists. The diagnosis is that you and I are different on the inside than we are on the outside.

> Woe unto you, scribes and Pharisees, hypocrites! because ye build the tombs of the prophets, and garnish the sepulchres of the righteous, and say, If we had been in the days of our fathers, we would not have been partakers with them in the blood of the prophets. Wherefore ye be witnesses unto yourselves, that ye are the children of them which killed the prophets. Fill ye up then the measure of your fathers. Ye serpents, ye generation of vipers, how can ye escape the damnation of hell?

What was Jesus trying to do when He struck out so forcefully and played a role that was really not Him, except on a few occasions, such as the cleansing of the temple? How can we relate to a history lesson that happened some 2,000 years ago? Who can give us the proper diagnosis of our condition today? Can we be our own doctor?

One time I decided that a member of my family needed a glucose tolerance test. So, I called up the medical center and said, "I would like to have a glucose tolerance test ordered."

And they said, "Who is your doctor?"

I said, "I beg your pardon."

"Who is your doctor?"

"Well, I didn't know I needed a . . ."

"Yes, you need a doctor."

I wanted a glucose tolerance test for a member of my family because of something I had observed with someone else's family. And they quickly reminded me that they are not in the business of allowing people to make self-diagnoses.

Yet the Bible says that when it comes to our spiritual needs, each one should examine himself or herself.

You mean I can get myself on the table and examine myself?

Yes, but notice what it actually says in 2 Corinthians 13:5 (paraphrased): "Examine yourself whether you be *in the faith*." Maybe there would be another way of saying it. Examine yourself, whether you're in touch with the doctor and trusting him, or whether you're simply trying to handle your own problems. Examine yourself, whether you are in connection with the One who understands the heart, because the human heart is deceitful above all things and desperately wicked.

There is a heavenly being who is directly in charge of helping us with the diagnosis. You read about Him in John 16:8: "When he is come, he will reprove the world of sin, and of righteousness, and of judgment." His initials are H. S. And perhaps you can guess who He is—the Holy Spirit. He penetrates to the inward parts and takes a look at what makes us tick.

As we look at this chapter we can get an idea about the symptoms of spiritual schizophrenia. I wonder if any of us will identify any of these symptoms personally, or if we can see them in our history, or even in our own church. Let's go back to the beginning of Matthew 23:3, where we find one of the first symptoms: "All therefore whatsoever they [the leaders] bid you observe, that observe and do; but do not ye after their works: for they say, and do not." They say and do not. They know how to say the right things, but apart from Christ they are incapable of really doing right. Verse 4 says that "they bind heavy burdens and grievous to be borne, and lay them on men's shoulders; but they themselves will not move them with one of their fingers." So, the person who is a victim of spiritual schizophrenia is a fanatic who imposes his own ideas on other people, but deep down inside does not really follow what he is trying to impose on others.

Verse 5 says that they do "all their works ... for to be seen of men." A great deal of front-and-center syndrome, if you please. "Watch what *I* do." That's a serious symptom of this disease.

Verse 6 says that the Jewish leaders loved "the uppermost." We could stop there, but it lists them: "The uppermost rooms at feasts, and the chief seats in the synagogues, and greetings in the markets, and to be called of men, Rabbi, Rabbi." So they are self-centered and love to be in the limelight, the uppermost seats.

Take a look at verse 13. What is the net result of people who are victims of spiritual schizophrenia? "Woe unto you, scribes and Pharisees, hypocrites! for ye shut up the kingdom of heaven against men." One of the definitions of the kingdom of heaven, or the kingdom of God, or the gospel of the kingdom, is the good news of salvation through faith. In fact, substitute *righteousness by faith* whenever you read the word *kingdom*. They keep people from understanding it. This is what the schizophrenic leaders are known by. "Ye shut up the kingdom of heaven against men."

Look at verse 14: "Woe unto you, scribes and Pharisees, hypocrites! for ye devour widows' houses, and for a pretence make long prayers." This is an interesting symptom.

They are known for long prayers. Maybe this is their way of trying to make up on the outside for what they lack on the inside. And maybe that's what Charles Spurgeon understood when he got up during one of his elder's long prayers and said, "While our brother finishes his prayer, let's sing number 563."

We find another symptom of the spiritual schizophrenic in verse 15: "Woe unto you, scribes and Pharisees, hypocrites! for ye compass sea and land to make one proselyte, and when he is made, ye make him twofold more the child of hell than yourselves." So, the person who is a victim of this disease and is a leader in the church is a great church-growth specialist. He loves to proselytize and get converts and more converts. He does not lack in that department. But in the end his converts become twofold more the children of hell than he himself is. Jesus called such religious leaders foolish and blind.

There's another area that spiritual schizophrenics are known for. From verses 16 to 22 Jesus talked about an intellectual argument that these people had gotten into concerning the temple and the gold of the temple. Evidently they were great at dissecting and analyzing. In other words, give them some intellectual hors d'oeuvres to talk about concerning religious things, and they could spend hours in what we might call pseudo-intellectualism. Another element that shows up here is inconsistency. The Pharisees were great on emphasizing minor things and neglecting major things. Jesus was making a call for real heart religion and consistency in the Christian faith.

Now we notice something rather startling about this disease. Verse 23 says, "Woe unto you, scribes and Pharisees, hypocrites! for ye pay tithe of [the smallest things]." So they were great tithe payers. If you want a church that has no money problems, look for a church full of spiritual schizophrenics. But there was a problem: They had no mercy, justice, or faith—or should we say, love was the big missing element. They were great on outward religion but lacking on the inside. And their biggest lack was faith and love and mercy.

So much for the symptoms and the diagnosis. Let's get to the treatment! Because the treatment is extremely important.

We already noticed in verse 26 that the treatment includes the need to "cleanse first that which is within the cup and platter, that the outside of them may be clean also." My brother and I learned, when we used to wash dishes, that we did not have to work on the outside. By the time we got the inside clean, the outside was clean. We couldn't miss. And this is the answer. This is really a challenge to the modern theory of behavioral modification. It's a challenge to the idea that if you don't feel loving, act that way anyway. And if you act loving long enough, in due time you'll begin feeling that way. The plan of starting on the outside and working in has always failed and always will fail. Only God is big enough to handle the inside. We can't do it. In fact, it requires surgery—major surgery. Which means you have to go to the doctor, to the surgeon. You have to go to the hospital.

And what is the surgery that it requires? A heart transplant!

I went to visit a man who was going to have a heart transplant one time. This was in the early days of heart transplants, and the risk was high, very high. I asked, "Do you realize the risk of what you're going into?"

"Yes," he said, "but I've decided that if I have to go on living the way I feel, I would rather not live." So bring on the risk! When a person surrenders to the hospital, surrenders to the surgeon's knife, and goes all out for a heart transplant, he has given up on himself. Right? That's why Jesus said, "They that are whole need not a physician; but they that are sick" (Luke 5:31).

I'd like to go to a physician, especially for a delicate surgery, who knows what he's doing and maybe who has known a little bit about what it's like to walk in my shoes.

There was a doctor in Bakersfield, California, who had never been sick a day in his life. Then he got valley fever. It hit him really hard. In the process, he actually ended up crippled. In fact, he had almost died. But after it was all over, I was talking to him one day, and I said, "This must be a terrible thing that you've been through."

He said, "It's the best thing that ever happened to me."

"What do you mean?" I asked.

He said, "Now, when I go to the office, I understand people who are hurting. I never did before."

Isn't it good to know that we have someone who understands how we feel because He was in all points tempted like we are (see Hebrews 4:15)? He understands, and He is the doctor. He is the great physician. He didn't have to have a heart transplant Himself, but He knows the bumps and bruises of a world of sin. He has "walked in our moccasins," as they say. He knows what it's like to take us to Ezekiel 36:26 and fulfill the promise, "A new heart I will give and a new spirit I will put within you." We go to this physician only when we give up and realize that He is able. And we can go to Him just as we are. We can stop trying to put Band-Aids on our cancer. We can stop trying to patch up ourselves when we are willing to admit our condition. Maybe that's why Psalm 51 is so clear on this. David, who had his share of struggles, became open and honest. He admitted exactly what his problem was and made a plea to the Great Physician to heal him. We too can go to this Physician for cleansing. "The blood of Jesus Christ cleanses us from all sin" (1 John 1:7). And in the surgery we have new blood.

I went to the White Memorial Hospital one time when

I was pastoring in Los Angeles, and Dr. Wareham invited me to watch heart surgery. I thought surely I would faint, because I had fainted once, just watching a film sponsored by the nurse's club at La Sierra University. But I got so fascinated watching the heart surgery that I didn't have time to faint. Dr. Wareham just stood there while others "did their thing"—the heart-lung machine, opening the chest, opening the heart. Finally, we saw the constricted valve beating out there in the open. And then came Dr. Wareham's part. He took the knife and began moving with the heartbeat, like someone trying to adjust tappets on an engine. He just barely touched it, and it opened a little. He touched it again, and it opened a little more. Then he put his knife down. He was done with his job. And everybody else was glad to let him do it. He was the professional.

I got so fascinated by this that I stayed in the hospital the rest of the day and visited all kinds of surgeries. A craniotomy, a mastectomy, an abdominal surgery, where all they could do was sew the person back up because of the tumor. And as I watched them, I couldn't help but think of the Great Physician and how we can trust Him. We can put ourselves in His hands and expect that we will come off more than conquerors as He deals with our case.

Well, what about postoperation? I wish I could assure you that you will get well and never have to go to the hospital again. But the truth is that you and I need to stay in the hospital the rest of our lives. And the hospital is the church. We go there to get well and to stay well. "Oh," you say, "I think I can get along without the hospital." But God says we can't! If we leave the hospital, the prognosis is terminal. We don't leave the physician either. We stay with the physician. And if we stay with the physician, we can expect a total and complete cure that will last forever. That's the way it is.

"Oh," you say, "I don't have enough money to stay with the physician and to stay in the hospital. Don't you know what has happened to medical prices these days?"

The world has indeed gone off and left us. I get sick just thinking about getting sick, because who can pay for it? Even the insurance payment is a problem. We're getting to where we can't even pay for that. And there is no such thing as life insurance. That's a misnomer. Why do they call it life insurance? There is no insurance company in the world that can insure life. All it can ensure is a rich widow. If there were an insurance company that could really insure life, there wouldn't be space to contain all the people who would be lined up waiting for it, right? So, how much is this going to cost?

Well, you know the good news. It costs nothing. Yet the bad news is that it costs everything. And you know how that goes. This treatment costs nothing, and it costs everything. It costs nothing in terms of dollars and cents. But it costs everything in terms of surrender and coming to the realization that we need Him and that we need the church, the body of Christ, in order to deal with our disease. There is no discharge from the doctor or from the hospital. And if we think there is, the case is nothing but terminal.

Listen, neighbor, I would like to emphasize the good news: that we are in good hands if we choose to put ourselves in the care of the Great Physician. But if we don't, there is no hope.

I'm also glad that when I have a problem I was born with, which is hereditary, spiritual schizophrenia, I can go to a doctor who is not a victim of the same disease. If I have psychological problems, I don't want to go to the ungodly for help. The Bible says I'm a fool if I do. And the mind games that are being played on people today are scary. I would like to go to our Maker, who understands all about the human mind, because "the heart is deceitful above all things. . . .

Who can know it?" (Jeremiah 17:9). I want the One treating my disease who can look into the deep recesses of my heart and help me understand what's wrong and what to do about it.

The experts have found out, I am told, that one of the causes of schizophrenia is poor nutrition. That was a big surprise to me. But it also explained how the wife of a friend of mine actually ended up in a state institution. They didn't know what to do until they got involved in nutrition and blood sugar and discovered this to be her whole problem.

Did you know that apart from proper nutrition you and I will have a relapse in our spiritual condition? Jesus said, "I am the bread of life" (John 6:35). And the Holy Spirit is spoken of as "living water" (John 4:10). Once again we are reminded of the simple remedies for physical and spiritual health: the sunshine of God's love; water—the Holy Spirit; rest—"Come unto me . . . and I will give you rest" (Matthew 11:28), of which the Sabbath is a symbol; air, which is prayer, the breath of the soul; exercise—Christian witness and service; and proper diet—God's Word. Then there is temperance or self-control, which comes only from God; and there is trust in divine power.

Why do I waste time and money when I have physical problems and I'm not paying attention to the eight natural remedies? That's not very smart. And why do I want to go to a worldly, secular—shall I go so far as to say ungodly— counselor, when I am not even paying attention to the heavenly counselor? Why waste all the time and money? I might need to, I might have to, and in my frame of mind I may have no other choice. But the appeal, physically, and spiritually, and emotionally, is to the Great Physician. I invite you to call on Him, and I invite you to invite your friends to call on Him, as we remember all that He wants to do for us.

The Woman at the Well—Part 1

Chapter 7

The Woman at the Well—Part 1

G o back with me 2,000 years and join me with the woman at the well. Let's try to find ourselves in the picture.

"Then cometh he to a city of Samaria, which is called Sychar, near to the parcel of ground that Jacob gave to his son Joseph. Now Jacob's well was there" (John 4:5, 6). In fact, it's still there. Did you know that? It's one of the few authentic places today that still exists somewhat as it was back then. Of course, they have a church built over it. (They have built a church over everything except the Sea of Galilee!) You can go down to the basement of this church and sit on Jacob's well. You can look down more than a hundred feet to the water below. And, if you choose, you can drink from the cup that two million other people have tasted from. Or you may choose not to! But, there it is, still today. Jacob dug that well when there was plenty of water around from springs and other wells. But apparently even in his day there was the problem of property rights and boundaries. So to avoid conflict, he dug this well.

The Bible says that "Jesus therefore, being wearied with his journey, sat thus on the well: and it was about the sixth hour [or noon]" (verse 6). Are you glad that Jesus got weary? He came to bring help to those who understand what it's like to have been born on the wrong planet. And

He knows what it's like to get tired, whether it's in a boat on the sea or at Jacob's well. We're not exactly sure why He was more tired than the rest of the disciples. All we know is that they left Him there alone, completely weary, and went into town to get something to eat. Apparently He couldn't go on. Or maybe He felt that a divine appointment was about to happen. In any case, we see Him sitting on the well when "there cometh a woman of Samaria to draw water" (verse 7).

This was not the most desirable type of one-soul audience in the days of the temple at Jerusalem. In the first place, women were not that high on the priority list back then. But Jesus came to place value upon women in a very special way. Again and again He did it. I preached a series on this one time and didn't know it would take five Sabbaths to complete it. But Jesus had a special regard for women who were the outcast and downcast ones in that society.

Another thing that made this a less than ideal one-soul audience was the fact that she was a Samaritan. Samaritans were called heathen and dogs by the people at Jerusalem. No self-respecting Jew would think of talking to a heathen from Samaria. To add insult to injury, this woman was probably not a member of the home and school board in the little village of Sychar. I doubt she was a leader of the parent/teacher organization, and it's quite unlikely she was on the city council. In fact, she had to come almost a mile away from town to draw water, because the other watering places, where the rest of the women gathered, did not afford her a place of security. She was *persona non grata* around there. She had had five husbands, which was not the most popular thing to do in those days. And the one with whom she was living at the time was not her husband.

So it's a surprise to us as we look on at Jacob's well to see

Jesus start talking to her. "Jesus saith unto her, Give me to drink" (verse 7).

Give me a drink?! What do you mean? He is the One who invented water in the first place, the One who was in charge of the water works in the desert with Israel. This One sitting there asking for water is the One who knows about the waters above the firmament and below the firmament. He's the One who can cause water to come out of a rock. With the snap of His fingers He could have turned Jacob's well into Old Faithful geyser. But instead, He is living as a human, just as you and I live. And He's at the mercy of whoever comes along for a drink of water.

Jesus never performed a miracle in His own behalf or for His own needs. That's why He said, "Give me a drink." He had another purpose in mind in asking this woman for a drink. It wasn't just that He was thirsty. He was using a method of service and witness that is very effective. People today are disenchanted with organized religion and our oft-used methods of witnessing. In fact, some of us cringe when we think of the typical old-time way of trying to get all the church members out knocking on doors of people they've never met before. We have so many stereotypes of witness. The new thing is to make witnessing a way of life. We call it lifestyle witnessing, in which we are witnessing all the time. It's not just a program. It's a way of life. But we have trouble learning how to do that.

A friend of mine went into a filling station one day, and the proprietor came out to pump gas. He said to my friend, "How is Jesus treating you today?" My friend was surprised. He didn't know what to say. Finally, he found words and said, "Well, never better." As he went on his way he thought to himself, "How can he do that so easily?" We're not used to that. But Jesus gives us a simple example. He asked a favor. And when you ask someone for a drink of water, it might not be long before they ask you for a drink of water. That's exactly what happened here at the well. Asking someone for a favor awakens trust. It's the Master at work, teaching us how to reach out to others. "Can I have a drink of water?"

> Then saith the woman of Samaria unto Him, How is it that thou, being a Jew, askest drink of me, which am a woman of Samaria? for the Jews have no dealing with the Samaritans. Jesus answered and said unto her, If thou knewest the gift of God, and who it is that saith to thee, Give me to drink; thou wouldest have asked of him and he would have given thee living water (verses 9, 10).

"If thou knewest the gift of God." Here we come to a central portion of this scripture. Jesus had arrived on the scene when one of the biggest problems that had plagued humanity from the beginning of religion was at its height among the chosen people. You earn your way, you work your way to heaven. It's not free. And the people who have enough backbone and muscle are the ones who can make it. Righteousness by muscle, righteousness by heredity, righteousness by temple worship. But all of it has to do with "You do it yourself."

This is the abscess that plagues all world religions. In fact, that's the great difference between all the rest of the world's religions and Christianity. It's amazing how it has jumped into Christianity as well. You don't have to waste your time investigating all the world's religions. It's pointless. All you have to do is remember one principle: just about every world religion has to do with saving yourself, while Christianity says you need a Saviour. The rest of the world's religions are based on merit. The Christian religion is based on a gift. God is on the gift system.

You'd think we would welcome that, but we don't. Everywhere people are obsessed with wanting to do something to be worthy, to deserve it. We wouldn't think of giving our boys and girls money for Pathfinders. We make them ride their bikes for half a day. (If the shoe fits, we'd better wear it.) That's the way we think: "—a-thon" this and "—a-thon" that and "—a-thon" the other thing. We are replicas of the people in the days of Christ. And He came to hit that system. He says, "If you knew the gift of God . . ."

At first glance we might think of all the things that are gifts in the gospel, such as: Repentance is a gift. That comes as a surprise to some of us. Forgiveness is also a gift. You can't earn it. The Holy Spirit is a gift. Justification is a gift, with all that it includes.

But what Jesus really had in mind was something that showed up a few verses earlier in John's gospel: "For God so loved the world that He *gave* His *only Son*" (John 3:16, emphasis supplied). *He* is the gift. Philosophical and theological ideas can help us understand. But *He* is the gift, and *He* brings all the gifts with Him.

"If you knew the Gift."

"Oh, I know about the gifts," you say. But do you know the Gift? Are you acquainted with the Giver? The One who came to show us that salvation is free? We don't earn or work for *any of it*. Yet how the world has gone on grinding away toward its ultimate demise, which sometimes seems just around the corner, and all the time we don't understand that all of salvation is a gift.

I'd like to propose that understanding this is the biggest problem for Christians today. That was the problem in our church in 1888. That was the problem in the 1890s and the twentieth century. We have a hard time receiving the gift. In 1988, which was the 1888 centennial, there were a number of articles written about the problem of 1888. One little short piece, in my judgment, makes everything else go to the back seat. We don't have to go so deep and come up so dry. This little piece is something that boys and girls can understand. I think it is outstanding.

The Trouble With Grace

A tough truth for nice people.
by Deborah Anfenson-Vance

Grace can be a problem. The Bible, in fact, brims with unsettling stories that show how grace again and again upsets the applecart as we know it. Big brother stews when Dad throws a party for a money-grubbing runaway who, down on his luck, has come home. Full-time employees grumble when the boss pays all his part-time workers a whole day's wage. Ninety-nine sheep are left at risk while a shepherd searches for *one* that is lost.

Now I might find these stories funny, even useful, if I happened to be the runaway son, the part-time worker, or one lost sheep. But a high-achieving, denominationally educated, church-employed, fourth-generation Adventist can hardly be typified by such terms. There's too much of that old-time religion coursing through my conscientious, good-kid veins.

So I catch myself sympathizing with the older brother, the full-time worker, and the ninety and nine. Even though I've heard these stories seventy times seven times and know their punch lines like Mother's voice. Grace seems against me and I am not amused.

Good people who take these stories seriously may see that part of the trouble with grace is that it doesn't take good people seriously. At least not as seriously as we take ourselves.

Which brings me to another point: Grace is troublesome not only to the legalist, or religious person. Grace can be tough stuff even for ordinary nice people to stomach. And if you want to go one further, I will say this: There is something about human nature in general that makes it hard for any of us to hold out an empty hand. Because if we did, grace would fill that hand. And what could be more troublesome than that?

Gifts are a problem to us. We are disciples of the make-your-own-way, the pull-your-own-weight system. We are capable, self-reliant, high-achieving. And we are guilty. We believe, deep down, that we don't deserve anything we haven't worked, suffered, or paid for, and we narrow our eyes at the free-lunch crowd. For all of our talk about giving, more often than not we mix the reality with trade and obligation; it embarrasses us to take a gift when we have no way to pay it back.

Accepting an out-and-out gift is tantamount to charity, which from childhood nice people learn is good to give and bad to take.

But if polite people have difficulty taking grace as the gift that it is, we also have trouble with the way it turns our good order on its head. We believe in white hats and black hats, and we don't like the way grace seems to mix them all up and, more often than not, let the wrong hat ride off with the princess into the sunset while Mr. Deserving stands sniffling alone at the unfairness of it all. There is something untamed about a God who would sponsor that sort of end to the show. It is obvious we have not yet successfully civilized Him to our sense of justice and propriety.

I could mention many more problems grace poses, but I'm going to stop here and go instead to another story Jesus told. Even *Jesus* admitted that grace could be problematic.

"No one sews a patch of unshrunk cloth on an old garment, for the patch will pull away from the garment, making the tear worse. [You cannot put righteousness by faith onto righteousness by works successfully.] Neither do men pour new wine into old wineskins. If they do, the skins will burst, the wine will run out, and the wineskins will be ruined. [You have to be a new creature; you have to be born again to appreciate righteousness by faith.] No, they pour new wine into new wineskins, and both of them are preserved" (Matthew 9:16, 17, NIV).

So in the meeting of old and new, we may recognize that the trouble with grace is the trouble with us. We are old shirts for new cloth, old vessels for new wine. [We are] too proud for the gift.

But grace also comes to elder brothers, and with it a choice. We may hold on tightly to life as we think it should be, cling to what makes us believe we are good, and do the thing that makes sense to our vision and has all along.

Or we can follow the hard and apparently senseless words, "Whoever tries to keep his life will lose it, and whoever loses his life will preserve it" (Luke 17:33, NIV) and open ourselves to grace, believing it will give us something beyond the shredded rags and the burst containers, though we haven't the foggiest idea what that will be.

And I myself cannot say what that will be, because it is the nature of grace to surprise.

One more thing I can say: We who let go of our righteousness, and lose our lives, will gain a new view of these unsettling stories. We will see ourselves lost in a herd of ninety and nine, prodigal in our elder-brotherliness, and chronically late to our full-time jobs. Then we may know a Shepherd, a Father, a generous Boss. We may find our lives and laugh at the unexpectedness of it all.

For as surely as we know ourselves lost, we shall be found. Found by a grace whose business is not to make good folks better, but to search out wandering ones and take them home. Take them home to a party.*

That's what Jesus was trying to tell the woman at the well. Will you join her there? It's a good place to be, because the well is too deep apart from His grace.

---

* Copyright by Deborah Anfenson-Vance. Used by permission.

The Woman at the Well—Part 2

Chapter 8

The Woman at the Well—Part 2

T here are three death sports commonly known among sports people: sky diving, scuba diving, and rock climbing. Rock climbing invaded our family through a teenage son who, as he got into college, kept wanting to do the bigger ones. His mother prayed for a broken leg before the climbs became more severe. But one day he and a physician friend were climbing Middle Cathedral, opposite El Capitan, in Yosemite. It was a two-day climb, and they were to sleep out overnight hanging in ropes on the sheer rock, twice as high above the ground as the World Trade Center in New York.

Unfortunately, they made some serious blunders. On the first day they dropped their canteen, and dehydration set in. When they finally made it over the top of the rock the next day, the doctor, who was a little older and more wasted, lying on his face, said, "Water, get water! Money is no problem, just get water!"

Our boy stumbled and crawled his way to a creek, buried his face in the water, and managed to get some back to the doctor. They discovered, to their surprise, that they had lost more than twenty pounds on the climb, and they were fortunate to come out alive.

"Water, pure water, that sparkles so bright, beautiful, fresh, and free." We don't realize what it's like until it's gone. Water is what makes you thirsty when the well is dry.

I remember being in the Middle East with Elder H. M. S. Richards, Sr., on his last Holy Land tour. We were in upper Egypt, where water was at a premium—pure, clear water. It was interesting to see all these Adventists drinking Pepsi Cola and jesting about taking their baths in Pepsi Cola. We each had a bottle of water. My bottle dropped in the airport in upper Egypt, and I exclaimed, impulsively, "My water just broke!" I never heard the end of that one. But if you travel overseas in some of these countries where you're frightened to death over the "revenge" of their particular culture, water is something that you cry for. You say, "Give me water, or I die." That's why the story of the woman at the well, which we began in the previous chapter, is something that comes to life when you consider your own experience of seeking water.

We have noticed that Jesus asked the woman at the well for a favor, and it wasn't long until she asked Him for a favor. Now He said, "If you knew the gift of God and who it is that says to you, Give me to drink, you would ask of him and he would *give* you living water" (verse 10, emphasis supplied). We've noticed that this is one of the major keys in the content of this story—salvation is a gift.

Yet, even though it's free, salvation still costs us everything. How do we get that together?

I recently read an article by a godly preacher south of the border, one Carlos Ortiz, who said it rather effectively:

"Jesus, in Matthew 13, told of the kingdom of God, and likened it to a merchant looking for pearls. And when he found a pearl of great price, he sold everything he had to buy it. Some Christians think the story means we are the pearls, and Christ had to give up everything to redeem us. But we understand, rather, that *He* is the Pearl of great price. We are the merchants seeking for happiness, for security, for eternity. But when we find Jesus, it costs us everything. He has happiness, joy, peace, healing, security, eternity, everything. So we say, 'I want this pearl. How much is it?'

" 'Well,' the seller says, 'it's very expensive.'

" 'But how much?' we ask.

" 'A very large amount.'

" 'Do you think I could buy it?'

" 'Oh, of course. Everyone can buy it.'

" 'But didn't you say it was very expensive?'

" 'Yes.'

" 'Well, how much is it?'

" 'Everything you have,' says the seller.

" We make up our minds. 'All right, we'll buy it.' We say, 'What do we do next?'

"He says, 'What do you have?' He wants to know. He says, 'Let's write it down.'

" 'Well, I have ten thousand dollars in the bank.'

" 'Good, ten thousand dollars. What else?'

" 'That's all, that's all I have.'

" 'Nothing more?'

" 'Well, I have a few dollars here in my pocket.'

" 'How much?'

"We start digging. Let's see, 'Thirty, forty, sixty, eighty, a hundred, . . . a hundred and twenty dollars.'

" 'That's fine. What else do you have?'

" 'Oh, nothing! That's it.'

" 'Where do you live?' He's still probing.

" 'In my house. Yes, I do have a house.'

" 'The house too.' He writes that down.

" 'You mean I'll have to live in my camper?'

" 'You have a camper? That too. What else?'

" 'I guess I'll have to sleep in my car.'

" 'You have a car? Two of them? Both become Mine. Both cars. What else?'

" 'Well, You already have my money, my house, my camper, and my cars. What more do you want?'

" 'Are you alone in this world?'

" 'No, I have a wife and two children?'

" 'Oh, yes, your wife and children too. What else?'

" 'I have nothing left. I am alone now.'

"Suddenly the seller exclaims, 'Oh, I almost forgot. You too. Everything becomes mine: wife, children, house, money, cars—and you too.' Then he goes on: 'Now listen, I will allow you to use all these things for the time being. But don't forget that they are mine, just as you are. And whenever I need any of them, you will give them, because now I am the owner.' "

That's how it is, when you are under the ownership of Jesus Christ.

So salvation is a gift, but it costs us everything. That's too big an order for many people. It's too much for the carnal heart. And that leads us to the realization that this story about the woman at the well is a story about conversion.

Unfortunately, conversion is a big neglected topic in the church. I am going to remain frustrated until we find out more about the great theme of conversion. After forty years of trying to talk about the gospel, it is disconcerting to discover that we know practically nothing about conversion. Yet in one sense this is the beginning point and the entire basis of the salvation experience.

I went to my library searching for materials on conversion. I have fifty-five volumes of Charles Spurgeon's sermons—big books that include every sermon he ever preached. I have volume after volume of the great preachers and great preaching going back 2,000 years to the early fathers. And I discovered that the amount of material on conversion is comparatively nothing.

"Well," we say, "the Bible itself doesn't say much about

conversion. It tells us that 'the wind bloweth where it listeth.' We cannot understand the wind, neither can we understand conversion."

But we'd better try harder to understand it! I want to know what it means to be sure I am converted. I want to know that people I work with are converted, to know how to reach young people who need to be converted. I want to know what it means to be converted again tomorrow and the next day, until Jesus comes. There are big questions we ought to understand.

Maybe for starters on the subject of conversion, we can get into this story a little further. You will recall that the woman said, "What was good enough for the fathers is good enough for us" (see John 4:12). That's an old moth-eaten argument.

Then Jesus said, "If you drink of this water you'll thirst again. But whoever drinks of the water that I shall give him, shall never thirst" (verses 13, 14). It was at this point that "the woman saith unto him, Sir, give me this water, that I thirst not, neither come hither to draw" (verse 15).

Notice the progression in the woman's way of addressing Jesus. She began by saying, "How is it that You, a *Jew*, ask something of me, a Samaritan?" A few minutes later she said, "*Sir*, give me of this water." Here we see the phenomenon of conversion taking place. May I suggest that the first step in conversion, or in coming to Christ, is a desire for something better? And Jesus was awakening this desire.

The woman had had this desire for a long time. She had been looking for a better husband—for five of them—and she was now with someone who was not her husband. She'd gotten tired of the vows and the ceremonies and was going to make sure before another vow. She was not satisfied. Her water pot, sitting on the edge of the well, is simply a symbol of the fact that the cisterns of this world do not satisfy. It's all right to look for pure water. But, if we are looking for the water symbolized by this water pot, then it is an endless search, like Ponce De León in Florida.

"Sir, *give* me this water." She is beginning to get the message. It's a gift. She's beginning to realize something that is very important. When you ask someone to give you something, you are admitting that you cannot produce it. You cannot earn it. You cannot deserve it. You can only ask for it. It's a gift. She's beginning to follow with what Jesus was teaching a whole nation and has been trying to teach the world ever since. Salvation is a gift. Peace and happiness are gifts. Immortality is a gift.

At this point Jesus said, "Go call your husband."

Suddenly things got really quiet around that well. She got sweaty palms, I'm sure, and she began a side step, a maneuver around the question, because she was afraid He would probe deeper. She said, "I have no husband."

Jesus said, "You're right. You've had five."

And then the woman said, "Sir, I perceive that thou art a *prophet*."

Here again we see the progression of the way she addressed Jesus. The conviction was deepening that she was dealing with someone more than the average stranger. So she comes in with her fancy footwork: "Which is the right church to go to?"

That's what happens when the Holy Spirit comes down hard on the sinful heart. God is not pushy, but He is persistent. And she responded by saying, Let's talk about something concerning the history of our people.

The Samaritans, as you know, were the product of intermarriage between Jews and pagans during the Babylonian captivity, and they were at great enmity with the Jews. They had rival temples. But the Samaritan temple had been struck with disaster, and at Jesus' time it lay in ruins. They also had rival mountains of worship, and a point of common discussion was where the best place was to go to church.

At this point, Jesus did something that is very meaningful, even for us today. This is more than a history lesson. It is real life for us now. He said, "It doesn't matter *where* you worship. It's *how* you worship that counts." And then He said these interesting words, which were something of a prediction: "The hour cometh, and now is, when the true worshippers shall worship the Father in spirit and in truth: for the Father seeketh such to worship him. God is a Spirit: and they that worship him must worship him in spirit and in truth."

Listen, friend, there is a big difference between being religious and being spiritual. There is a big difference between knowing the rules and regulations and standards and dogmas of the church (while beating that heavy path between your house and the front door of the church) and *knowing God.*

God is a Spirit. A mathematician once told me that God lives in another dimension. There's nothing new about that, of course. And if we could see into the next dimension, as Elisha's servant did, then it would all become clear. The only person who can worship God in Spirit as well as in truth is the one who has become spiritual. And the only One who can effect that is God. The method by which He does it is called conversion. And it was happening that day by the well. It was happening with a one-soul audience.

That to me is exciting, because the same regard Jesus had for that one, He has for you and me today.

Is there anyone who has a desire for something better? I do. Is there anyone who has an understanding, a little understanding of the knowledge of the plan of salvation, the gospel? You do. That's why you are reading this book and why you like to talk about these things. Is there anyone who understands that it is a gift that we cannot earn? It comes only from God. His well is too deep for us, apart from His intervention. And is there anyone who will join the woman at the well, realizing their sinfulness? We're not just talking here about the usual kind of sinner. There is a worse kind. Conversion means to turn, or to turn around. And there is a different kind of turning around than simply from our usual sins. It could be that for third- and fourth-generation church members, the turnaround is the turning from our own righteousness to His righteousness. And the last I checked in the book called *Steps to Christ*, that is the hardest one to experience.

It is easy for God to reach sinners, harlots, and thieves of the usual order. It is very difficult for God to reach proud people who have been "doing just fine, thank you." "I wouldn't think of committing an immoral act. I am a good person, God. Take care of the drunk in the gutter. And keep Your stars and planets from crashing into each other. But, I am a good person. I don't need You." That's the big one! The miracle of conversion can happen only when we turn from our own righteousness and our own goodness to the goodness of God. And that is the only kind of goodness there is. Isn't that true?

Then we notice this woman coming to the point of surrender, because when Jesus talked about spiritual things, the Holy Spirit took her the next step.

For a long time Adventists have talked about the "the truth." Now I am getting into my own subculture. You've heard of it. Our grandparents "came into the truth" eighty years ago. We found "the truth" in South Dakota. I accepted "the truth." May I remind you that "the truth" without the Spirit isn't worth a dime? God isn't looking primarily for people who know the truth about distinct points of doctrine. He's looking for people who know Him, who is the Truth, the Way, and the Life (see John 14:6). And He's looking for people who have mercy and love.

Ron Halverson said it well at a recent camp meeting: "The problem with the gospel is that it's good news. If it were bad news we would have been happy to pass it on, and the work would have been finished a long time ago." God is looking for people who see in this Stranger at the well someone they would like to be like in terms of mercy and love.

When Jesus got to this point, the woman said to Him, "We know that the Messiah is coming." Something was trying to resurrect itself in her memory. She had studied in her quiet moments the literature of her ancestors, and she knew about the Christ, the Messiah who was to come. She said, "We know He is coming. And when He comes He'll tell us everything." And then Jesus did what He didn't do at the temple in Jerusalem. He said directly and simply, "I that speak unto thee am he."

That's all it took! The woman left the well immediately. She left her water pot (and that's not a bad idea; let's leave *our* water pots), and she went to the city, because she had something to tell.

Here's something interesting about the genuine Christian witness: No sooner does a person come to Christ than there is born in his heart a desire to tell someone else what a precious friend he has found in Jesus.

This woman was in the presence of someone who could "tell her everything she did." It was an overstatement. He hadn't. He had only told her about one small part of her life. But it's like the lightning that strikes in the dark of night. It hits only the oak tree, but everything else is illuminated at the same time. She was impressed by this. She rushed back to town to tell the men. (Very interesting! It says that she told the men. The women had quit listening to her a long time ago.) She told the men, "Come, see a man, which told me all things that ever I did: is not this the Christ?" She had moved from "a Jew," to "Sir," to a "prophet," to maybe the "Messiah," and now "the Christ."

We're all impressed by the spectacular. If someone came along and told us everything we ever did, we would be impressed. We had a group of students at La Sierra University several years ago who got involved with the charismatics, the "glossolaliacs" in Los Angeles. They'd go into town, thirty or forty of them, and some of them would come home "slain by the spirit," stiff as logs, carried out by their friends. Something was happening, and they were impressed because someone who was a complete stranger could sit down and tell them all about their lives and their problems and their sins in detail. They said, "This must be supernatural." It was. But, which spirit? Just because something is supernatural doesn't mean that it is of God. And just because the stranger at the well can tell me everything I've ever done doesn't prove that He's the Messiah. There were other proofs that thrilled her heart. There is something more important than being told everything you've ever done.

There are going to be people at the end of the thousand years (and a little bit longer from now) who will stand in the presence of One who can tell them everything they ever did. There will be millions on the inside of a giant city of dimensions we cannot fathom, a multitude that no one can number. And there will be millions on the outside from every generation. The people on the outside will stand watching as an audiovisual program comes on. You and I will see it on a great 360-degree screen high above God's throne, showing the whole story from beginning to end— the great controversy and where we fit in. Every human being will see himself or herself in the picture, and no one will move. On that day, it will be a tragedy to be standing on the outside, in the presence of One who knows everything we've ever done. But, it will be nothing but good news to be standing within, where all is covered by His blood.

That was the case of the woman at the well. She not only

met someone who could tell her everything she ever did, but she was in the presence of someone who loved her and was winning her to His kingdom. It's still true today, isn't it? For you? Come, see a man—the Man Jesus.

The men of Sychar followed her. Watch them as they come. Watch her running across the wheat fields toward the well again. Behind her are these men following, for other reasons this time. And they come into the presence of Jesus. Then we see something fantastic at the end of the story. It says, "Many of the Samaritans of that city believed on him for the saying of the woman, which testified, He told me all that ever I did." But notice verse 41: "And many more believed because of *his* own word; And said unto the woman, Now we believe, not because of thy saying: for we have heard him ourselves, and know that this is indeed the Christ, the Saviour of the world."

And that's the way it ended. Not only was He a Jew; not only was He kind Sir; not only was He a prophet; not only was He the Messiah; not only was He the Christ; but He was and is *the Saviour of the world.*

I am interested in this dear Saviour. Are you? I want to join the woman at the well.

The Grasshopper Complex

Chapter 9

The Grasshopper Complex

I am going to list ten names from your Bible, and I want you to identify them: Shammua, Shephat, Igal, Palti, Gaddiel, Gaddi, Ammiel, Sethur, Nahbi, and Geuel. Do you know who they are? They're in your Bible. Now we add two more names, and then you will know: Caleb and Joshua.

The reason we are not familiar with these first *ten* names is that they were victims of the grasshopper complex. And anyone with the grasshopper complex is not going to be heard of for very long in God's book. In fact, the public career of these men was really only about six weeks long. Then they died in a terrible plague.

The children of Israel were on their way to the Promised Land. They didn't take the short route, and they hadn't yet taken the long route. It had been about two years since they left Egypt, and they had spent some time around Mount Sinai. Now they had come up against the borders of the Promised Land, and the people came to Moses with an idea. Moses went along with it, but it was the people's idea. They said, "We're not sure we can take the land. We'd better send a committee of twelve to look it over." So twelve men were chosen, one from each tribe, and they examined the land for six weeks. They came back with a big bunch of grapes. They called a meeting of the congregation of Israel to present

117

their report, and the people were all expectant, excited, looking forward to the conquest of Canaan.

I don't know how many people were there. Estimates run all the way from 100,000 to two million. But there was a large assembly. And from the platform came two reports. The first was from the majority. They all agreed that the land was a land flowing with milk and honey. They agreed that the fruit was wonderful, and that it was an attractive place. But they said it was impossible to take the land. You can read the report of the ten in Numbers 13: "We came unto the land whither thou sentest us, and surely it flows with milk and honey; and this is the fruit. Nevertheless, the people be strong that dwell in the land and the cities are walled, and very great: and moveover, we saw the children of Anak there. The Amalekites dwell in the land of the south: and the Hittites, and the Jebusites, and the Amorites, dwell in the mountains: and the Canaanites dwell by the sea, by the coast of Jordan" (Numbers 13:27-29).

In the middle of this pessimistic report of the majority was a man by the name of Caleb who couldn't keep quiet any longer, because he saw the effect the report was having on the congregation. A steady rumble of discontent and adverse reaction had begun and was growing. So Caleb jumped to his feet. You can almost see him taking the floor. He interrupts with these words: "Let us go up at once and possess it, for we are well able to overcome it" (verse 30).

But Caleb was interrupted by the majority. "The men that went up with him said, We be not able to go up against the people; for they are stronger than we. And they brought up an evil report of the land which they had searched unto the children of Israel, saying, The land through which we have gone to search it, is a land that eateth up the inhabitants thereof; [Well, it hadn't eaten up the giants yet.] and all the people that we saw in it are men of a great stature.

And there we saw the giants, and the sons of Anak, which come of the giants: and we were in our own sight as grasshoppers, and so we were in their sight" (verses 31-33).

Right there the congregation began to cry. Everybody at the same time. I don't know what it would be like to hear two million people cry (or even 100,000), but it must have been a terrible sound. They didn't just weep quietly in their handkerchiefs. They wailed. They lifted up their voices and cried that night. Evidently the crying went on way into the night.

A committee, of course, is an object of ridicule even today. I heard one person say that the ideal committee is one of seven people with two absent. Someone else said that a committee of five usually consists of a dominant chairperson, three people who will say yes, and one who will consent to bring in the minority report.

The minority report of this committee was not the popular report. In this case, however, the majority were wrong. And when it comes to the things of God, the majority has always been wrong. Isn't that right? As far as the masses of people are concerned, we have a great warning, from Jesus Himself, that it's the broad way that leads to destruction, and many will take that way. It's the straight and narrow way that leads to life, and few there be that find it. So if you are going to be on God's side when this world is finished, you're going to be in the minority, not the majority. That's why the fact that an organization that appeals to the multitude is not any proof of its validity. It is proof that we ought to take a second look. Yet "majority vote" is what the world is based on at large, even in its advertising. "Do what the crowd does. Follow what the majority says."

Do you remember those signboards all over the country advertising Acme beer? The signs showed the pictures of different types of people, and the assumption was that they covered all the population, which was supposed to show that everyone drank Acme beer. "Railroad engineers do . . . They drink Acme beer." "Office secretaries do . . . They drink Acme beer." They even had a nice little old gray-haired grandmother sitting in a rocking chair with the words "Little old grandmothers do . . . They drink Acme beer." And you were supposed to immediately rush out and buy a case of Acme beer because "everybody's doing it."

I remember Virginia Proctor Napier, in the art department of La Sierra University at that time, coming up with a poster for the temperance contest. It was a hobo, with red eyes and bewhiskered chin, sitting on a railroad car, and she wrote underneath, "Hobos do it . . . They drink Acme beer." She got first prize.

You're on the wrong side when you base your opinion on the opinion of the majority. Here they were in the days of Israel, wrong again. And all the people cried, and they began to say certain things that sounded like prayer. One of them was, "Would God we had died in the wilderness" (chapter 14:2). God heard that, and He answered that prayer. It's an example in the Bible of prayer answered against God's will. Did you know that prayer has sometimes been answered against God's will?

Another thing they said was, "Were it not better for us to return to Egypt?" (verse 3). And a group of them got together to hurry back to Egypt to the taskmasters and the garlic and the onions. There was big trouble in the camp as the wailing went on. But amid the wailing and the noise of the discontent in the camp we see two men who did not have the grasshopper complex. They were Caleb and Joshua, and they ran among the tents and among the people. They shouted above the tumult: "If the Lord delight in us, then he will bring us into the land and give it to us. [After all, wasn't it the *promised* land?] Only rebel not ye against the Lord, neither fear ye the people of the land, for they are bread for us. ["We can eat 'em up!"] Their defense is departed from them. The Lord is with us. Fear them not" (verses 6-9).

But all the congregation said, "Stone them! Stone them with stones!" And they grabbed for the stones, raised their arms to let Caleb and Joshua have it, when suddenly there was a brilliant flash of light. People looked toward the tabernacle of the congregation, and there was the obvious evidence that Someone, who had beheld the whole scene, was manifesting His glory in the camp. There was nothing to say now. They'd already said too much. The ten spies with the grasshopper complex crouching low began to creep toward their tents. The people held their breath. A plague broke out in the camp, and the ten faithless spies were the first to go. But not Caleb and Joshua. Their names have gone down in history, and the echo of their courage still brings the thrill of excitement and adventure and hope to troubled hearts. "We are well able, if the Lord delight in us."

Go way back in time. There are eight people, the minority again, getting on board a boat in the days of Noah. You see Daniel and his three companions. Just a handful, a minority, who did not have the grasshopper complex. You see a man by the name of Jacob who goes down to Egypt to visit his son before he dies. And he walks into the palace and says, "King Pharaoh," as he raises his hands and places them on his head. "The Lord bless you, king." That seems a strange thing to do. Usually you let the king put his hands on your head to bless you, but not Jacob. With the presence of God in his life he was not awed by the ivory palace or carved lions in the throne room.

You see another man who lives in the wilderness, and he comes out once in a while and mingles among people. Then he starts preaching down by the river. And the crowds come out to listen. He stands erect and fearless in the presence of King Herod. Why? Just one man with a lone voice in the midnight darkness of the time before Jesus' first coming. What makes the difference? He realizes that God is bigger than all of them, and he is not awed in the presence of earthly dignitaries.

You see another lone man in a garden, and you see disciples leave Him. You see Him between two thieves. Before this experience at Golgotha He had been on a hill just over the way, the Mount of Olives, and He had said to a handful of followers, which included a few humble fishermen and some women, that the day would come when His gospel would go to all the world. There wasn't the slightest proof or evidence that it would take place. One Man, who was also God, apparently alone, forsaken by everybody—at the cross.

It wasn't any easier for Israel at the end of the forty years to face the same giants their fathers had faced. In fact, by then there were more giants. They'd probably had a population explosion in those days, just as we do. And during that forty years these giant women had been giving birth to giant fifty-pound babies, and the babies had grown up. In addition to that, these people no longer feared God's people because God's people had done something disastrous after their sentence in the wilderness. First they said, "We won't go in even though Caleb and Joshua said we can." And then, when Moses let them know that God had heard their prayer and they were going to die in the wilderness, they said, "Well, now we'll go in." It almost reminds you of Johnnie and the beans, you know: Mama says, "Eat your beans."

And Johnnie says, "No, I'm not going to."

So Mama changes her tune and says, "Don't eat the beans," and Johnnie eats them. I know. I've had it happen at our house. This is the kind of people these Israelites were. They said, "*Now* we're going to go up. We're going to do what God said. We're going to take the land. We'll fight the inhabitants." But that is where they were wrong. God never told them to fight. In fact, it was the land of *promise*, and you don't have to fight for something that's promised. That's one of the big lessons that people still need to learn today. We don't have to fight for something that's promised. Has God promised you and me victory, personally and individually? How many of us are still fighting for it? Could it be that that's the secret of our defeat?

They said, "We'll go and fight." They went up, disorganized, a great, unwieldy band of people. They said, "We'll overpower them just by our numbers." And they rushed at the enemy, but they came back bruised and bleeding. The next night the whole camp cried again except for those who were lying still on the field of battle. They wept and they cried, "You mean we must die in the wilderness?" That's right. Because of the giants. They are stronger than we are. We can't do it.

Now thousands of years have gone by, and we come today to the time when we are again at the borders of the Promised Land. Do you believe that?

"Well," someone says, "how long can we be on the borders? Haven't we been on the borders for a hundred and fifty years?"

Evidently so.

Someone says, "Christ is never going to come, and we'll never see the Promised Land until the 'character of God is perfectly reproduced in His people.'" Then they take a look at the people, and they say, "Relax, there's plenty of time."

Someone else says, "He will never come until the gospel is taken to all the world." Then we come along with the statistical report of population growth versus the work that's being done, and we think, "Relax."

Someone says, "He will never come until the majority of

the people in church get busy—start doing their work." And they take a look, and they say, "Relax. Five percent is not the majority. We have plenty of time."

Listen, neighbor, I'd like to remind you that if you'll study carefully you'll discover that Jesus is going to come again whether we do our work or not. Jesus is going to come again whether we carry the gospel to all the world or not. It's nothing but ego that has led us to believe that the whole thing hinges on us. Do you realize that? God has other ways of getting the majority on His side than waiting for the majority to get on His side. All He would have to do to make a majority is to shake up and cut down the total number far enough, and there would be a majority. Some of our human ways of trying to figure out how it's going to happen will be answered very simply.

As to the people who are going to have God's character reproduced in them, our misconception has been to think that six million people are going to have this experience. That's not necessarily so. I believe the reason why the children of Israel finally went into the Promised Land is clearly portrayed in the book of Deuteronomy. If you read it closely, you will discover that they finally went in, not because of anything they had done or because of anything they had become. They went in, in spite of themselves, and because of the people of the land of Canaan, who had filled up their cup of iniquity. That's why!

Let me ask you, has this world just about filled up its cup of iniquity? The evidence is overwhelmingly Yes. Revelation tells us that Jesus is going to come and destroy those who destroy, or corrupt, the earth (see Revelation 11:18). And if I am ready then, then I will be ready. If I'm not, I am not.

"Oh," someone says, "how can I get ready? It sounds as if maybe it's a little closer than some of us thought." So we take a look at our lives, and as we look, we see giants. We see things in our lives and in our hearts that are stronger than we are—pride and the love of the world, impurity and temper and gossip and impatience. We look at these giants, and the more we look at them, the bigger they become. We lash away at them futilely in our human effort, and we say, "Oh, they are stronger than we are." And we begin to develop the grasshopper complex in our personal experience. I don't think that story in the Old Testament was written just as a history lesson. I think it says something to each of us in our personal lives.

So don't get the grasshopper complex! Don't begin looking at the giants, because when you look at the giants you look small. It's true that the giants are stronger than we are. My impatience and my temper are bigger than I am unless I am the strong-willed, backboned kind of person who has been able to control his external acts. But this would harden me forever against needing God and needing Christ's power. The truth is that whether we are strong or whether we are weak, on the inside everyone is at the same level when it comes to needing and accepting the message of Caleb and Joshua.

Do you feel in your own sight as if you're a grasshopper? Stop looking at the giants. Stop looking at the things that have troubled you. Stop becoming a backslider and giving up gradually on the church and on religion. Stop dragging the standards of the church down to meet your level of performance.

When we look away from the giants and begin looking at Jesus, begin looking to God and His power, the grasshopper complex begins to fade away. The Lord delights in us. Is that true? Does He still delight in us? Does He still love you? Are the friendly words of Jesus, "Come unto me, all ye that labor and are heavy laden and I will give you rest" (Matthew 11:28)—are these words still good for today? Is the Scripture truth still worthwhile? "Who shall separate us from the love of God?" (Romans 8:35). Is He still smiling upon you, my friend? All the words of the Bible say that He is. And if you look at Him, then the giants begin to look small. That's the premise, and that is the beauty of salvation through His strength instead of yours.

Now, you don't have to fight for something that has been promised. This was one of the misunderstandings of the Israelites. They said, "We will go up and fight" (Deuteronomy 1:41). Deuteronomy 3:22 has clearly pointed out to us that God never intended for *them* to fight. "It was not His [God's] purpose that they should gain the land by warfare, but by strict obedience to His commands" (*Patriarchs and Prophets*, p. 392).

I remember making a bicycle for my boy one Christmastime. It was a special order. They never made that kind in any shop anywhere. It had to have a certain kind of handlebars, a certain kind of wheels, a certain kind of gearshift and fenders. I had to custom-make it for him. I worked on it for hours, and finally out in the garage on Christmas morning, there was the bike, all ready to go. I was hiding behind some things there. And as he came out to look at his new bicycle, do you think he had to fight to get it? He *didn't* have to fight to get it! It was a gift from his dad. And he would have had to fight *not* to get it! You don't fight for a gift.

Let me ask you, my friend, has God promised you and me victory through the power of Christ in our lives? "Thanks be to God, which giveth us the victory" (1 Corinthians 15:57). "Faithful is he that calleth you, who also will do it" (1 Thessalonians 5:24). A lot of people are discouraged today. And the reason is that they are looking at the giants. Don't do it. Don't do it! "Oh, but *I think* the giants are too big!" *God says*, "They are not!"

We've gotten the idea that we have to look at the giants. Someone quotes, "Ye have not yet resisted unto blood, striving against sin" (Hebrews 12:4). But we've forgotten that the writer understood that you do that by looking to God, by drawing nigh to Jesus.

"Well," someone says, "We have nine volumes full of rebukes of sin. *We* ought to work on them."

No! The only reason why "God rebukes His people for their sins, [is] that He may humble them, and lead them to seek His face" (*Review and Herald*, 25 February 1902). That's all. God doesn't get after us for our problems and our faults to get *us* to work on our problems and our faults. He gets after us so that we will ask *Him* to work on them.

God never revealed the giants in the land of Canaan to the Israelites to get them to fight the giants. His purpose was to drive them to their knees. It was Joshua who spent the night on the floor of his tent before a battle in which God took the lead and brought down hailstones that gave His people the victory. So let us get "to the floor of our tents," on our knees, like Joshua. Let's accept the words of Paul in Philippians 4:13: "I can do all things through . . ." Whom? Through trying hard? No. "Through Christ who strengthens me." Down with the grasshopper complex!

"Oh, but look at the person across the aisle. He did me wrong years ago, and I am discouraged." Stop looking at the giants. There may be giant hypocrites. God never invited you to look at them.

"Oh," someone says, "I am dying of a terrible sickness." Stop looking at the giants. "Oh," someone else says, "I am lonely. I've lost a loved one." "I have a family that's broken up . . . or breaking up."

Don't look at the giants. Sure, they are stronger than you are. Stronger than I am. But God is stronger than all of them. Aren't you thankful for a Saviour who has promised us all the power of heaven and in earth—for a God who still can reward the faith of people like Caleb and Joshua?

Present Truth in the Real World

by
Jon Paulien

In the ongoing struggle between Christianity and secularism, who's winning? Is the world becoming more like the church, or is it the other way around? How can a church founded in the 1860s compete for the attention of today's secular person?

In this explosive book, Pastor Jon Paulien identifies the task of reaching secular people with the everlasting gospel as the most urgent challenge facing Adventists today. When reading this book, you'll discover:

- Who secular people are and how they think.
- How to meet their felt needs.
- How to live among and work for them without losing your own Christian experience.

This book is too important to pass by. Get yours today!

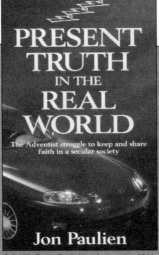

US$10.95
Cdn$14.80

Available at
your local
ABC, or
call toll free:
1-800-765-6955.